I0491477

O'Studios 'Zines Index
Volume 4 – 1969 – 2019
Ritchie Mined Series – 2nd Edition

O'Studios 'Zines Index

Volume 4 – 1969 – 2019

Ritchie Mined Series – 2nd Edition

Compiled by Nellie Sunderland nee Ritchie

Copyright 2020 Bill Ritchie

Ritchie's Perfect Press

500 Aloha #105

Seattle WA 98109

Preface to O'Studios

Of thousands of retired art professors, Bill Ritchie may be the only one outside of Wikipedia which a browser can dig into a professor's imaginary place and read hundreds of titles, summaries, and images of his unpublished essays. They are real, but the island of Open Studios and Hospitality is virtual, a figment of his imagination.

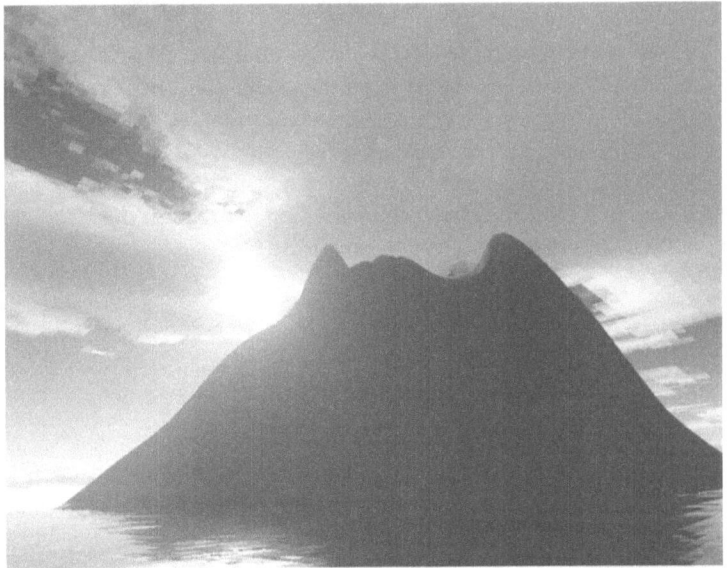

View of Open Studios and Hospitality, O'Studios, on the Great Lake of Emeralda Region – one of Bill Ritchie's imaginary places.

He is like a castaway on this imaginary island. In this make-believe world of Emeralda which he created in the early 1990's, ten islands lie on a great lake and in cabins on each one are located libraries where 'Zine indices in paperback and eBook are stored for future reference. With the help of one of his daughters, Bill offers his chronology of O'Studios' Zines, 568 summaries of essays from 1969 to 2019. Their full text is stored on their computers and are shared on the cloud.

Emeralda's O'Studios

Bill Ritchie learned ten things a person ought to experience to understand and practice printmaking – Bill's *Domain-of-Expertise*. He learned printmaking is the ancestor of all the media arts. Photography, film, television, and computer graphics descended from print. These "grandchildren of printing" gave all we know in science, technology, engineering, and math and, by the way, art.

When he was at the university teaching fine art printmaking, the era was afire with new ideas in all those areas and Bill was drawn to new technologies. He envisioned a new curriculum for printmaking. Partly it was because he shadowed his students when they graduated into their informal, post-graduate work. He walked in their boots, one might say, partied with them, worked in the same art studios, and shared their highs and lows.

He learned that expertise in *Open Studios and Hospitality* is one of the requirements for a successful art career. Readers may detect the implied importance of sociability, i.e., the ability to be socially involved, scattered throughout this index of summaries.

When he left the university in 1985, Ritchie's habits of research, note-taking, journalizing, and essay-writing were deeply ingrained. This was the beginning of a new kind of educational experience and a privileged time when keeping an index can be a work of art.

Foreword

To students, are their professors' libraries special? Maybe a library would satisfy some students' curiosity if wondering, *what kinds of books do their professors own?* Can a student get insight into the professor's teaching by seeing what books they keep?

Anyone's private library reflects the owner's mind, somewhat. For example, browsing someone's library and finding a compendium of children's stories alongside a biography of Dylan Thomas, one might wonder: *How do these connect?*

Or, in their physical arrangement, books arranged in neat, alphabetical order reflects something about the owner's mind, too. In the character of a professor's library one might influence a student to become a professor. It happened to me.

Access to my professors' libraries in the 1960's helped me become a professor. I'm passing this experience forward. Read more about my experience in the Afterword at the end of this book / eBook.

- **Bill Ritchie, Seattle 2020**

O'Studios 'Zines

os690127
Disappointment and depression
The Fulbright failure

His application for a Fulbright to stay in Norway a full year has failed, but the experience of making the application was worthwhile. His wife is pregnant, which makes the prospect of studying with Rolf Nesch more pressing. There are options, such as a … 213 Words.

os690417
Proving my plate in Norway
Journal entry

The author writes about wearing an extra T-shirt and sweater and receiving a thermos and some smørdrød from the house lady before walking to Nesch's studio. He writes about the humorous way of etching outside in the snow. 198 Words.

os690427
Leaving Nesch and looking back
Journal entry

The author writes about his last day with Nesch. Nesch wanted to buy one of his prints, regarding it as an obligation to sell him a worthy print after returning to Seattle. The author feels bad about the proof he made that day. 468 Words.

os690606
A set of drawings and Krishna Reddy
Journal entry

The author shares his thought about making a set of works entitled by numbers. He also writes about his meeting with Krishna Reddy and his wife Judy and going to the Desjobert lithography printing workshop. 509 Words

os700507
Not prepared for politics
Journal entry

He writes in his journal that he never thought his journal would be filled with the politics of college art school. He makes a claim that education is more important than industries, and vows to put education before everything else for the sake of his an… 329 Words.

os701218
Readying for a show
Journal entry

The ink for his print, "Stones with Knees," referred to as S&V Transparent base is given as something that he thinks will be useful for other printmakers to know about. He lists his progress in readying for his upcoming one-man show at the Seligman Gall... 147 Words.

os710216
Prospects for a talk and demo
Journal entry

"Tomorrow," he writes, he will go to Pacific Lutheran University to give a talk about his artwork and do a demonstration. "All is going well on all levels," he begins, and describes the beehive of activity in Room 4 at the UW, and without his being there... 226 Words.

os710226
Evolution of Resolution Letter
A thank you sample

This is a thank you letter from Mr. Coke. It also announces the next catalogue coming out later that year that will be of interest if following the planned exhibition titled "The evolution of Resolution." This is a selection from the folio. 292 Words.

os710307
Looking forward to April
Journal entry

The artist/teacher began keeping a journal in 1968, prior to his first trip to Europe (with his wife) where he studied with the renowned artist, Rolf Nesch. His journal entries are intermittent—sometimes with entire months passing by with nothing written. 313 Words.

os730118
A visit to a high school
Journal entry

Today he goes to give a talk at Lake Sammamish High School about his art, but at home a letter is waiting for him to mail of worrisome nature, and he thinks the end of his teaching printmaking is coming. He has started using video – what does it all mean? 177 Words.

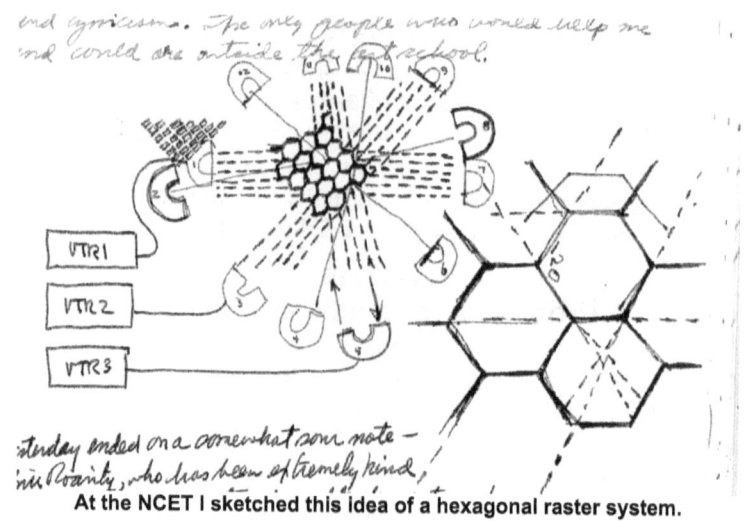

At the NCET I sketched this idea of a hexagonal raster system.

---

os740216
At the National Center for Experiments in TV
Journal entry

He's been awarded an internship at the National Center for Experiments in Television and describes his hours. It is not all happy, as he records his frustration with the other interns from Seattle's public television station. Brice Howard and the other ... 816 Words.

os750328
A warning dream
Journal entry

Are dreams worth anything? Should one give dreams credibility as anything other than what one's brain might do when it's bored? While the other parts of one's body needs rest and hours to rebuild and restore worn-out cells, does the brain dream for entertainment? 816 Words.

os750616
Dreamer
A Short Story

The author of this story re-discovered his original 1975 manuscript and reviewed it in 1991 and 1993. It is his autobiographical fantasy, about a man re-entering society that is starting over, without the benefit or encumbrances of recorded world history. 2220 Words.

os760526
Gene Baro visits Triangle Studios
Journal entry

It was a big day for a few artists is Seattle today because the print department director from the Brooklyn Museum visited on a hunt for prints to exhibit in this prestigious showcase. This entry describes the event and sidelights to his experiences at t... 1430 Words.

os760903
Art Review of Akira Kurosaki
By R. M. Campbell

This article is a review of Akira Kurosaki's show at the Erica Williams Gallery. The article describes Kurosaki's work with combining woodcut and photography. He studied with Bill Ritchie while staying in Seattle. 374 Words.

os770517
Valuation of video art and printmaking
Journal entry

The day previous to this, he experienced an awakening, realizing that he wanted to insulate himself against further shocks of the internecine handling of the graduate program. Contrasted with the exciting prospects of deeper involvement with video, printma... 465 Words.

os780517
Media and the self
Journal entry

He was thinking that every aspect of life, including life itself, could be taken away from people and sold back again, the single distinction of humanity that set it apart from this earth and that this propensity had been set in motion by human reflection. 523 Words.

os790507
On living and working space and computing
Journal entry

He speculates on the notion of buying into a downtown Seattle loft as a live/workspace, wonders about the future of Triangle Studios – now three years old – and by the end of the day he's been given an Apple II+ desktop computer to use for his own thing. 608 Words.

os790825
Malraux and Beginnings of Media Arts Language
Journal entry

The author describes the book "The Voices of Silence" by Malraux as interesting. The book declares that there is a language of painting, as unique as the language of music. The author theorizes the idea of printmaking and media arts having a language. 401 Words.

os800416
Material, non-material and cybernetics
Journal entry

A graduate student questions why does one need to make material art if we are entering an age of non-material art? The author considers his reasoning from what he's read by Benjamin, Malraux and Marquez. It may be a convergence of architecture and computers. 1142 Words.

os810517
Sailing and Cyanotypes
Journal entry

He has enrolled in a four-day sailing school, and after his second day of lessons he returned to Triangle Studios and made two cyanotypes in the "Studies for Locus 3." He writes that the combination of sailing and art relate to the interactions of things.

os820507
Headed for the World Print Council
Journal entry

Invited to be one of the speakers at the World Print Council conference, "New Printmaking Technologies," he writes about his misgivings plus his excitement. He thinks of the stories that Leonardo da Vinci had music playing while labored on his paintings. 191 Words.

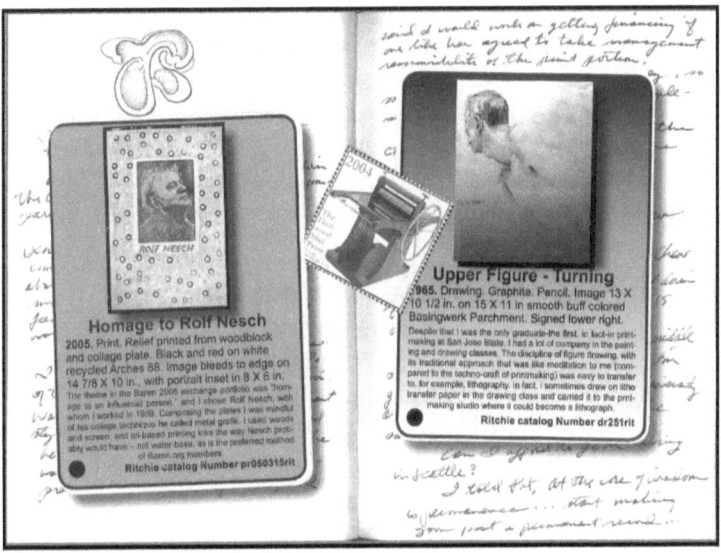

os830507
Last day in Paris
Journal entry

On his last day in Paris he visits Danny Bloch, at the Museum of the City, then the Ecole des Beaux Arts with his former student, Eric Katter. He showed his work to a mixed response. This lengthy entry is mostly about the video art showings he saw and qu... 1157 Words.

os840117
An unappreciative University
Journal entry

He tells an imaginary listener, "There's nothing else that brought out any better from me than the University. Yet, there's nothing I've ever encountered which has appreciated or even understood it less. I'll send another "enrichment" application to Beckmann." 176 Words.

os840206
A job of diminishing returns
Journal entry

It's a sad entry as he feels his interest in his job diminishing and becoming a boring task. He regrets that it could have been so much more if he had known how to combat the pushback against his ideas. He regrets that he underestimated their viciousness. 237 Words.

os850206
Hard times at Centrum
Journal entry

He's at an artist's retreat in Port Townsend at the Fort Worden State Park, an artist-in-residence. His situation at the UW Art School became so stressful he begged for an unpaid leave of absence and a small stipend and promise to publish came to take ...

os850517
"Art Prof uses TV for his Canvas"
UW Campus newspaper article

This article by Kurt Jensen discusses the new method of creating art; video art and home computers. The reporter includes quotes from Bill Ritchie explaining the enrichment that the use of the medium of television will bring to art, mentioning that MTV i... 1144 Words

os860417
A visit with Lisel Salzer, Linda Ferris
Journal entry

His visit one of Seattle octogenarian painter, Lisel Salzer, reminds him of working with Rolf Nesch. With Stevan Worley he visited Linda Ferris to convince her of testing the Internet as a venue.

Surprisingly, it was more encouraging to Salzer than Ferris! 320 Words.

os870117
Your Art There
Reconstructing the past

Having finished the first set of O'Studios 'Zines: Ritchie Mined in the year 2010 now the author can try using it against the original idea that these 'Zines could be useful in a serious game. He plays the Walter Cronkite card, renaming it Your Art There. 876 Words

os870216
Reflections from Lake Quinault
Journal entry

He is on a family retreat at their favorite place, a resort on the Olympic Peninsula by a lake. Having taught a month at TESC, he reflects on the structure of this school and how his early Central education compares in their press for excellence by goa ... 398 Words.

os880127
Personalizing Rifkin and Jantsch notes
Journal entry

A discovery in reading "Star Wars," by Jeremy Rifkin and Eric Jantsch, who describes behavior over the next age as behavior which enhances evolution. The author found the quote fitting a description of my goals...Understanding towards doomed opportunities. 555 Words.

os880206
Lake Quinault one year later
Journal entry

He's feeling good because, once again, despite the setbacks he and his family experienced, they are back at their favorite retreat, Lake Quinault Lodge on the Olympic Peninsula. He considers the response he got from Dennis Mashek about fine arts appli ...

os880216
Tale of A Blind Elephant
Who Knows What Computer Art Is? A Parable.

Adaptation of the story of the blind men and the elephant to provide answers to the question, "What is Computer Art?" The author is an artist who began his work with printmaking and worked up to video and computer art from there. He's a storyteller, too. 1461 Words.

os890117
Locus defined
Dr. Richard Brown's review of Ritchie's art

This is the text that was written by Dr. Richard L. Brown for a 1989 one-man art exhibit by Bill Ritchie. At the time of the show, Dr. Brown was the gallery director and the head of the Department of Art, Pacific Lutheran University in Tacoma, Washington. 467 Words.

os890805
Life among the Metaphors
The bitter and the sweet

An account of the highs and lows of life among the metaphors, an imaginary people. Their values are sometimes found in those living in the silicon forest. From the Emerald City to the Emerald Valley, life with the metaphors is bitter / sweet. 721 Words.

os900914
Positive Acceleration
Outline for patience

Three paragraphs describing the metaphor of the dripping faucet of life. 164 Words.

os900924
The Farmer and the Meritocrat
Looking down, looking up

An old division between agriculture and culture-culture is examined by a former farm boy who moved to the city. 227 Words.

os910616
What is Open Studios?
Excerpt from Ritchie's Inc. Business Plan of 1991

This text is from a business plan Bill Ritchie wrote to explain the structure of Ritchie's Inc. which was a C-Corporation, consisting of ten divisions. Open Studios and Hospitality was—and is—the division devoted to community outreach and public relations. 525 Words.

os911014
TESC 2011
Dreamer awake

Reading history from the view of a TESC-education, the fictional teacher grows conscious of the origins of the college itself. Basic tenets endured forty years of political and economic change, despite change in technology. 1523 Words.

os911103
Rings on water
Inspiration for mosaic

These words were written in a tiny notebook which Bill Ritchie discovered when he was cleaning his studio. During his design of an ill-fated mural for Spokane Community College, its message seemed to make more sense. 461 Words.

os911123
Teaching the next generation of printmakers
Accessing knowledge with new machines

Responding to an article by Hugh J. Merrill, the author asks where the new technologies will lead educators who want to teach the next generation of printmakers because discoveries in arts in 1991 connect printmaking with new media and water-sealed caves. 521 Words.

os920117
Cityland in Paintbrush
Portrait of A Museum of the Future

This might be a rough draft for another article; it has the appearance of a diary or a key-by-key record of a morning in the Perfect Studio, or, as this author refers to his muse he named "Media," it was written by the woman who fell to earth. 563 Words.

os920216
Masters and Fools
Being Your Own B.O.S.S.

Possibly the information age will see the revision of the old adage to "Who seeks a Master is a Fool." This article follows years of experimenting with a tool called by its manufacturer, the B.O.S.S., a palm-top electronic notebook similar to a computer. 1040 Words.

os920307
Confessions of A Closet Economist
Know Enough to Get in Trouble

Talk about economic trends and famous economic theorists pique the information technology person's interest if he or she can connect it with getting a job doing what they most love to do: Play with high-tech toys. 895 Words.

os920317
Ken's Golden Age
The Rolling Summer School

Conversing with Professor Ken ten renews interest in a fabulous Summer-school bus. The author paints a background for the technologically minded, creating edutainment in virtual reality and takes a strange turn into the realm of the soap opera. 4876 Words.

os920506
Did I See You on "First Thursdays?"
Hints to Art on the Data Highway of the Future

To promote the book, Art of Selling Art, this letter was sent to book review editors in the Puget Sound area. It is based on life in the gallery scene where most artists look for their livelihood. The truth is, few artists make a living, and this article asks journalists to comment on the situation. 857 Words.

os921228
Ola! Ohaiyo! Hello Media!
Concept for Media's KidsVid

Based on an announcement printed in a newspaper, this is a copy-written version of what might become reality. The computer revolution winds down, and arts education reform picks up. This program is as original as Sesame Street. 1650 Words.

os930107
Ride the data highway
An art store, a train

Excerpted from RIISMA Magalog:Art Classrooms of Tomorrow Today. The Art EarthSafe 2022 Class of the future is a multimedia, and these were part of the essay that mixed business, retail, hospitality, marketing and sales with real and fantasy events. 1215 Words.

os930117
A fun letter to Professor Eckre
Art and politics collide on the data highway

Was Professor Eckre being an absent-minded professor when he wrote a letter asking for free desk copies of my publications for his political science class in North Dakota? It's fun to imagine what he thought when he got this response. 324 Words.

os930415
Reading an art magazine from 2022
Loveletter to Media

He heard on the radio that media is responsible, but if anyone is to blame, it's us. That's why it breaks his heart and boggles his mind that people still - after all these years that media has been with us - do not see what is between virtue and reality. 689 Words.

os930206
Automated Library Machines
ALMS for the poor

As I unpack my electronic library of ToolBooks, I find projects partly unfinished. It was years ago when I first created these, yet they are intact. What would a stranger, skilled with browsing electronic ToolBooks, think of my crude sketches? 994 Words.

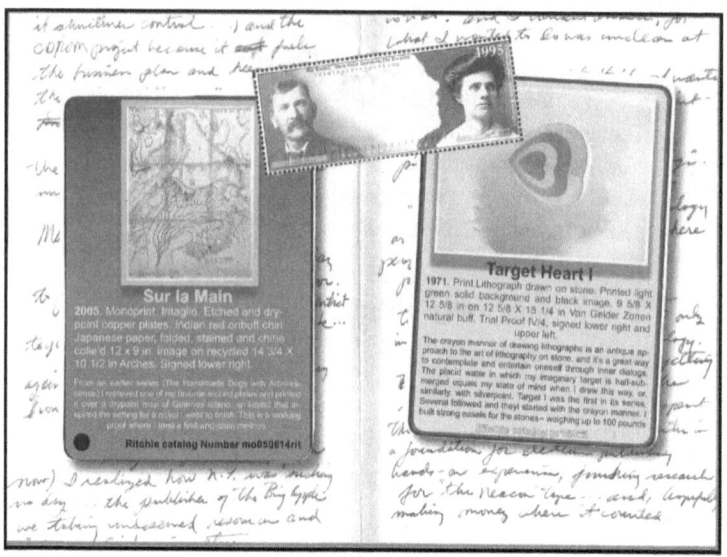

os930216
Valley dreamers
Blending the two Washington's

The author is roused from his computer dream-world. "How did I get here? What happened? Has the dream come true already?" He considers whether computer technology and agriculture will crest in the agricultural part of Eastern Washington State. 1553 Words.

os930308
Herstory
Script for the foyer

Collecting the numerous relations of Herstory (Media's) into a powerful crystalline lattice work and presenting them to a classroom of one-million students. 533 Words.

os930318
Postcards to a ghost in the machine
Postcards to my ghost

Short messages to a "ghost in the new machine." 317 Words.

os930328
I want my ITV
Surfing downtown

The artist, crafts person and designers can use ITV in ways that commercial stores might not want us to think about, but this article suggests that it would be better for creatives if they do. 1444 Words.

os930407
Three little pigs
Stories from Yakima

What Yakima needs is a story-telling monument to speak to the world about sunshine, food, fresh water and growing things. From this and the organization that maintains it the stories from many nations go out with every parcel of Yakima Produce. 505 Words.

os930417
Play Work
For mature interactives only

Thinking of an electronic game for two that is part Pictionary and part "Where in the world is Carmen SanDiego?", the author puts himself in the player's seat. Put the joystick in your hand and imagine this game you play on the data highway. 2170 Words.

os930427
Hit your wagon to a star
IT Professor on interview

The story of a another encounter the ITinerate Professor counts as "The 4th kind." Dependent on three industries (Transportation equipment, food processing and tourism) the educators / entertainers look for technology to move their information. 2216 Words.

os930507
US United States
Hor Story

The symbolism in the story of the luxury liner-turning-to-scrap-metal is prophetic. Reading that the 1952 ship, SS United States, was rusted and would be auctioned as junk, I began to make Her story into a focal point in "The Woman Who Fell to Earth." 438 Words.

os930517
One wish
Eve of an anniversary

It is the eve of my 29th Wedding Anniversary. In two days, someone might ask me, "If you had one wish that you think could come true here, what would it be? 868 Words.

os930527
Game roundtable
Dial "900" to get out

Reinventing arts studios began in the 80s after Naisbitt and Aburdene's "Reinventing the Corporation." An artist invented an inner board of directors for his projects and explains the diagrams of "Meeting of the Bored." This is the base for Emeralda. 385 Words.

os930606
Conversation of the Bored
Hours away from a life

The reader is asked to imagine ten clones of Bill seated around a round table, a crystal ball in front of each seat. They see the logo of each of Ritchie's ten divisions. This article is self-talk that guides the reinvention of arts studios. 1061 Words.

os930616
LUXury Club
Investment clubs are the answer

The author says ideas of Kenneth Lux, economist, need to be examined to find answers to investors' questions. The sustainable investor needs to know how plans fit the next thirty years. Track investment clubs: see how they find direction and growth. 1500 Words.

os930626
Narrative for a storyboard
Fit for a hard drive

Over time, the artist reinvented his studio to fit on a computer hard drive. For each division, images evolved that were icons for each division. Finally, a storyboard resulted that suggests a fly-by tour of the Perfect Studios. 1154 Words.

os930706
TRPI
The right stuff for investing

TRP Investment is a means of achieving financial, educational and social goals. A long-range plan, stretching fifty years into the future, makes TRPI an ideal way to invest time. How does one qualify? This article suggests some criteria. 222 Words.

os930924
Food co-op metaphor
Electronic peaches next?

This article suggests that the intellectual and social-emotional dimensions of the human personality can grow on the food co-op model by applying it through technology, the tools of the age of electronic reproduction. 2289 Words.

os931004
Cruising Virtual Reality
Fantasy coming about

Here is a whole-brain approach to members of the cruising industry to put art, education and technology into the picture of cruises. Content would be able to outperform most land-based settings with "Computer Arts Stars Theatre." 2505 Words.

os931014
What I want in a cruise
Letter to the liner

A member of a special segment of the "geezer generation" fantasizes on what he would say if a cruise industry poll asked him what he wants in a luxury cruise. It's not what you would expect from the nations' richest population. 1983 Words.

os931123
Interview with a data highway driver
Tight turns and steep hills

Six months after an interview with a new data-highway builder, the author asks, "What if I had answered differently? It might have been the crack in the doorway through which I could see the accomplishments I was seeking for the past eight years: The Perfect Studios." 1736 Words.

os940107
College in the palm of your hand
Gleaning education on your PDA

The new college course will be palmtop-based. The author stares into the tiny screen on his Casio B.O.S.S. and, like a crystal ball, it tells him the past and future of the Personal Data Assistant itself in education. A game called "Emeralda" is born. 509 Words.

os940117
Playing Emeralda
Future work for artists

You roll dice in the play of "Emeralda" not by using old die. Old game pieces and artifacts of the industrial revolution are good only as archaic metaphors. New tools unlock the secrets and are keys to invention of new solutions to old problems. Emeralda is the future workplace and includes artists. 216 Words.

os940127
Visualize Buying Rose Hill
A Media fantasy

How do you save an old wooden school from demolition when developers move in? Is there a profit center in historic preservation? A business plan is needed, preceded by a fantastic visualization session for visualizing heritage development business. 503 Words.

os940206
LMASOCACAD Quintet
Soul of the new museum

Five foci for a new living museum: One for text of all kinds. Another is for numbers. The third is for graphics. Fourth is sound and the fifth is called by various names such as telecommunications, electronic data transfer and data highway systems. 1280 Words.

os940216
Rose thorns of silica
Vision of a glass connection

After the author and his co-workers lost the battle to save Rose Hill Grade School, he occasionally goes back over his database and records for artifacts of the project. Better than any photograph of the lost school, his stories enliven his imagination. 933 Words.

os940226
Cruising your studio
Between virtue and reality

This article was copy-written while reading the tutorial for the world's first PC-based virtual reality planning software for personal architecture. Mouse in hand, or a grip on your joystick, you enter your studio and go to work 1458 Words.

os941218
Interview a PATCWA Student
The boredom of practice

Formatting an expert's unpublished articles is boring in this fantasy interview. The students at Pacific Arts and Technology College-Washington work for a small salary and dream of better methods. 1855 Words.

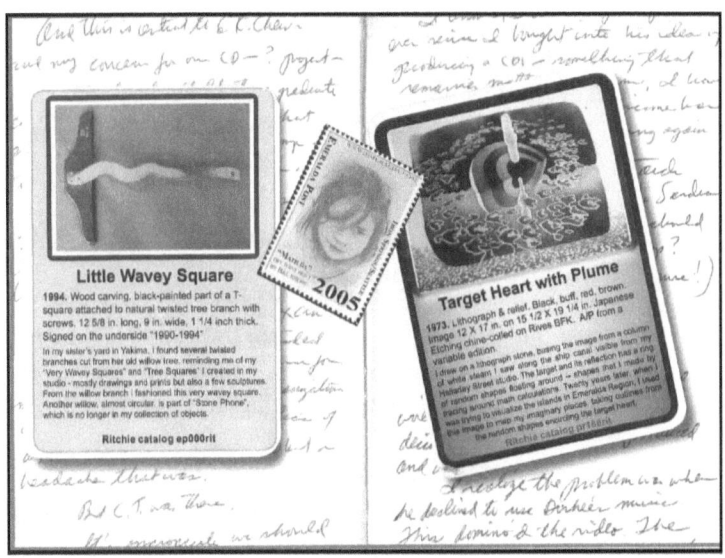

os950826
Living Prints Travels World Class
Reinventing free fine art printmaking

Having left campus, the ITinerate Professor sets course for a new way of looking at travel and study of fine art printmaking, conceiving a custom study tour business in which the leaders in colleges and universities meet their counterparts in business. 1041 Words.

os951103
A Gift to LMASOCACAD
Donor of portable video equipment

Received via e-mail November 2, 1995: An open letter by Mark Leonard who, with his wife and co-worker Izumi Kuroiwa, donated a 1983 video camera and recorder that Bill Ritchie used to make his Travel Tapes. Mark describes how the system helped Kuroiwa-Leonard Media Arts get started. 721 Words.

os951218
Land of Visionaries
Tech corps' Emeralda

They say you cannot name a Tech Corps chapter in Washington without approval from the national office in Washington DC, but maybe you can get away with naming one in an imaginary, sim state like my beautiful imaginary region, the city-state of "Emeralda". 3030 Words.

os951228
Symbolic Dream & Conversation with Living Prints
Journal entry

Notes recorded from the author's "palmtop" B.O.S.S. computer. He records a dream about receiving blank checks. He hopes of a customized studio. He did wood cutting & Lithograph online. He writes a description of his own book following other examples. 357 Words.

os960107
Perfect Work, Perfect Way, Perfect Service, Perfect Pay
Journal entry

Notes recorded from the author's "palmtop" B.O.S.S. computer. After reading Shinn's book, the author is convinced that he's talented and gifted that must be shared and grown. He accomplished completing his resume on his home page. 219 Words.

os960317
Visit to Open Studios and Hospitality
Cybernetic Isle with heart in Domains of Expertise

The fourth stop on a ten-day tour of the Domain of Expertise, a fictional lake where arts, technology and business are mingled in the atmosphere of a future search. Excerpt from Reinventing Arts Studios Workbook. 1883 Words.

os960406
Ritchie and the Witch
Little Mind Workshop Book

Four elements are joined in an entertaining story about a witch, a cat and a Master of Digital Arts, a story about how Dreams Work to produce a Mind-Blending of Napoleon Hill's "Think and grow rich" and Kevin Trudeau's "Megamemory." 828 Words.

os960506
A US Tech Corps Dreamer's Sketchbook
Flight of the 888 series

Created to encourage communications among people interested in arts, business, and communications technology education. The image of the airplane was contributed by Jerry Ritchie, and the mountains and sea of edutainment were added by the author. 644 Words.

os960516
Muralism in the age of digital communication
Flight of the 888 series

The outcome of this parable determine what, if any, is the common goal US West and AT&T Pioneers and Tech Corps Washington, as proposed by the first author, who filed an intent to charter Tech Corps in Washington state. 893 Words.

os960526
Carla, the virtual flight hostess
Flight of the 888 series

A telecommunications pioneer suggested the need for a partnership for an upcoming conference and discussion. Her invitation inspired the story, "Muralism in the Age of Digital Communications." 983 Words.

os960606
Fanciful approach to quality teamwork
Flight of the 888 series

Last in this year's four-part of a story created on-line for people interested in arts, business, and communications technology education by a visionary intent on chartering a US Tech Corps chapter in Washington state. 735 Words.

os960804
Alive and well among the metaphors
Life in the tall forest

Where I live there once stood fir and cedar trees that were so tall that no one had ever been able to climb to their tops. Living among such giants made people think big. The trees are gone, but their spirit remains, and that is why I think big. 1233 Words.

os960814
Roots of Emeralda
Search for life

Games fascinate the artist who uses electronic tools in his art and craft, but why? When a telecommunications company makes a deal with a game company, many possibilities are raised and point to a famous scheme called "The Glass Bead Game." 2656 Words.

os960824
Virtual Versus Vicious Games
Paths Toward Emeralda

Perhaps The Wizard of Oz is one of America's greatest stories ever told, and it is based on fear of the unknown and a Yellow Brick Road. The pathways to Emeralda is based on faith in the unknown and intuition. 647 Words.

os961003
Another perfect day
Scene at Open Studios & Hospitality

A Gruddite Apprentice-User (coming from MacRitchie's Fast Art) expands his mentor's directive, writing about a perfect day. It's almost time for exercise, but there's always time at O'Studios to do what one has to do to protect one's most valuable assets. 640 Words.

os970127
How to butter your bread on both sides
Churning your own HSIC portfolio

An old trick by unscrupulous stockbrokers is to churn the portfolios of unwary clients, skimming the commission on transactions that, in fact, are unnecessary. Churning your own portfolio might make sense even if you don't get paid for it. 1522 Words.

os970216
Is there a Martha among us?
Craft and ability in the cybernetic age

The well-known corporate craft queen is compared to Wiener, Rosenblueth and Thomas Jefferson because her helpful hints can be adopted to solving big-picture problems. It may appear simple, but it is not easy. 1053 Words.

os970308
Let the games begin
Planting the seeds of cooperation

Ritchie's game theory and economic modeling combine for educational uses of information and telecommunications technologies. Like seeds planted in a rich culture of human interaction, games, play and story-telling, they blossom in a jungle of opportunity. 2580 Words.

os970318
Dialing the Dead
Postscript to the underground

Random sampling of names from out of the past sometimes has a way of showing how fast things change, and in the passage of an entire year, unfinished plans seem to indicate a deadening effect has taken hold of some people. 1110 Words.

os970328
Beautiful horses
Parable of the Gates Prize

Keeping beauty in the gates of wisdom is like capturing wild horses in this parable by Bill Ritchie, whose Japanese-given name means "Keeper of beauty in gates" or, "Biru Richi". 435 Words.

os970407
In a printmaker's house
An artist copy-wrights a writer's words

An imaginary visit to the house of a printmaker in the cybernetic age takes the form of a dialogue with author Robert Grudin (On Dialogue, Book: A Novel) who, a decade before, used a similar approach to plumb the richness of his art. 1455 Words.

os970417
Emeralda's name and symbol
History and evolution

Considering that a trademark registration of the name "Emeralda" is forthcoming, a review of the origins of the name and its logo is in order. 951 Words.

os970914
An art show is born
Surprise outcome of economic modeling

Events from the 1970's and 90's led to Emeralda's Pacific Digital Fine Arts Festival. The show is simple on the surface, but its roots go deep into a concept of creating a new economic model for cyber artists. Selection from the "Reinventing Arts Studios." 1324 Words.

os971014
Interview with the inventor
Emeralda's Bill Ritchie

Fictional interview with the inventor of Emeralda: The Game For Life as the cybernetic artist/entrepreneur searches for ways to figure out what he is doing while he is doing it. 780 Words.

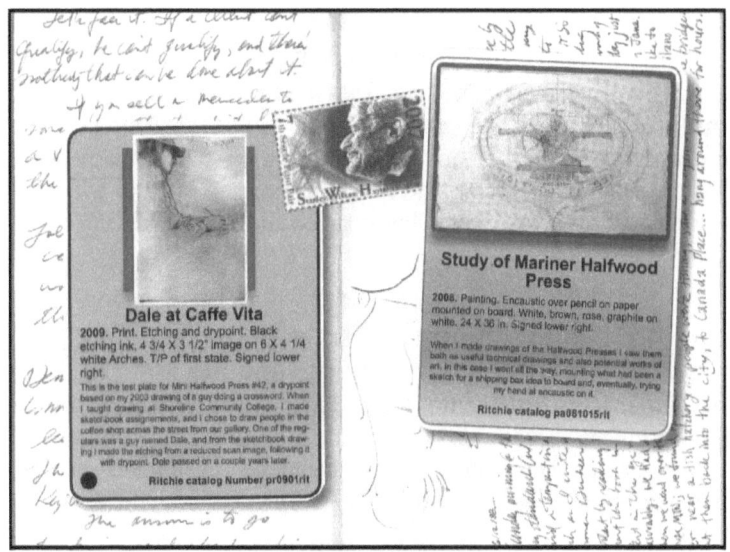

os971103
Stamp Evaluation
Emeralda's post

The Stamp game is a subdivision of Emeralda. This is a unique game. Because it is a subdivision of Emeralda, it is necessary to keep it in the context of the game itself. That means it has to be evaluated. Evaluation is the third step in six. 1556 Words.

os971113
Moving Graphic and Evaluating Stamps
Journal entry

The author writes his time log of the day, the activities and projects he did that day. He records moving graphics of Cyanotypes Stamps to .tif files. He records editing his article, Evaluating Stamps. He records notes from Denis Waitley from KXPA. 713 Words.

os971123
Grandfather clock
Poem of a prisoner

The author, who works alone with only the company of a mantle clock, is carried away for a moment by self-pity. 151 Words.

os980107
O'Studios Vision
Getting to the Destination state

Third day of a User Apprentice' Residence Stay at O'Studios and a language lesson, based on the pronunciation of the name of an obscure printmaking tool. She is part of a vision in the eye of the Emeralda Master who shares his story on the World Wide Web. 697 Words.

os980117
Legacy Transfer
High cost of living legends

The ways costs enter into the transfer of information are like engineering and economics welded into a basic theory for a new kind of investment. The author wants to invest in human structural intellect, one's ability to capitalize labor over a long term. 731 Words.

os980127
The festivals at Emeralda
Glass Bead Game Reborn

The inventor reflects on the development of the Festivals that take place that give masters an opportunity to demonstrate their strategies without seeming to be ingratiatory. 812 Words.

os980206
Explaining Emeralda
Stranded on a Desert Isle

The inventor of "Emeralda--Game for the Gifts of Life" thinks about himself in comparison to someone who has been stranded for 15 years and suddenly faces rescue. 1782 Words.

os980216
Flying over O'Studios
A Dreamer's Day

The author shares his first view of O'Studios Isle, the Domain-of-Expertise for outreach and community relations for artists, crafts people and designers. Flying high above the isle, he sees its shape for the first time, but he's confused by an old dream. 659 Words.

os980226
Emeralda Daydreamer
An Essay for Ellie

His friend, Eleanor Mathews, is on his mind as the author tries to communicate his invention, Emeralda. He pictures a print making studio and animates it with imaginary people with links to dentistry, computers, travel and investing. 2010 Words.

os980308
Economics of Product Development by Apprentice
First-day Notes of a Visitor to Open Studios and Hospitality

The Inventor-User is at the first day's lecture on the Island where entertainment and hospitality are supposed to be the reigning principles, but instead hears a management science specialist addressing the issues of the high cost of information transfer. 1099 Words.

os980318
Back story for Titanic and US
How the Titanic and the SS US crossed in the night

The creator of Emeralda: Games for the Gifts of Life, writes periodically in a story that is the background for the games. Every big game has a background legend or fantasy story. These are passages from it, set in Scotland at the beginning of the 20th C. 658 Words.

os980328
Aurel and Open Studios
Journal entry

The author introduces his entry with Aural being the dominant sister for that day. That day he was in the Open Studios domain, which he describes as a networking opportunity for artists. He discusses Emeralda players' pre-requisites for goals and visions. 646 Words.

os980407
Explaining Emeralda
The Master Speaks to Beginners

On the threshold of another new experience in a day in the life of the Emeralda Master poses the ongoing, inner dialog on explaining

Emeralda to his ghosts in the new machine. Pausing between virtue and reality, he adds more definitions. 1039 Words.

os980417
Interview with an email addict
Journal entry

A fictitious interview. The scene is a prison in Spain. They expect Sr. Augnendo. But he doesn't come. He's sent to Mondragon. He finds the skilled and knowledgeable unable to survive. He invents a strategy and the wisdom of his ways is contagious. 752 Words.

os980507
Free-style Writing for Emeralda Dummies
Demonstration 3 at Emeralda Works

Free verse is the style here as the Inventor of Emeralda writes down what he's thinking while role-playing for the Emeralda Interview tapes he'll be making in a few months. This essay is a document made on the fly while the author works on his puzzlement. 1389 Words.

os980517
The Billionaire's Game
Journal entry

The author writes about theoretical Heuristics with Hubris. What motives, or makes a billionaire want to move? The same force that moves them to act on the information they get (which is the same for everyone) matter more. Notes included from Wriston. 2060 Words.

os980527
Two short steps
Journal entry

The author writes thoughts and conclusions from reading three books. The authors of those books include Hesse, Wriston, and Hagel & Armstrong. He writes about the Information Standard, the Virtual Community and his contributions to these things. 2744 Words.

os980216
How do you play today?
Lost in the woods of O'Studios' Isle

A series of accounts for routine activities yields essays that resemble demonstrations by the Emeralda Inventor and Master at Play. In this account he begins with questions about the Cells in which he finds himself. In this instance, it is a virtual wood. 1184 Words.

os980527
Two short steps
Journal entry

The author writes thoughts and conclusions from reading three books. The authors of those books include Hesse, Wriston, and Hagel & Armstrong. He writes about the Information Standard, the Virtual Community and his contributions to these things. 2744 Words.

os980616
Smooth Moves in the Heart and Mind of the
Magister Emeralda's demonstration

A User Apprentice describes his final, sixth day at O'Studio's Residence Stay, when the Magister Emeralda appears and shows how smoothly he moves from one cell in the Vade Mecum to another. This demonstration previews what he must learn in the … 506 Words.

os980626
Three Kinds of Interference and their Effects
Searching for peace, safety and joy on Earth

The author met three comrades on a watercraft to consider strategic alliances to benefit organizations with common visions of peace, safety and joy on earth. He engraved their meeting date of on a blue water bottle-a letter of intent, a noteworthy effort. 781 Words.

os980706
How cells blend in Emeralda
Bed-and-Breakfast Games for the Gifts of Life

The inventor of Emeralda uses an example a listserv member (Baren-list) posted as a comment about staying in a B&B while traveling. The author, once an avid traveler who now prefers virtual travel, presents his thoughts based on memories and experiences. 1253 Words.

os980716
Outside the Box
Demonstration for squares, cells and handmade graphics

In the science of cybernetics, from which the game of Emeralda evolves, there is a clue as to what it means to play "outside the box writes the game's inventor, and here he describes a connection to Descartes, cartography and the prints of Mauritz Escher. 1413 Words.

os980726
The First Try of Printmaking On-line
An evening to remember at Daniel Smith Inc.

The writer looks back at a two-hour event he planned and produced at Daniel Smith Inc.-a Seattle art supply store-in which he inked, wiped, and printed an intaglio and chine-colle print, converted it to a digital file and got it to his World Wide Website. 374 Words.

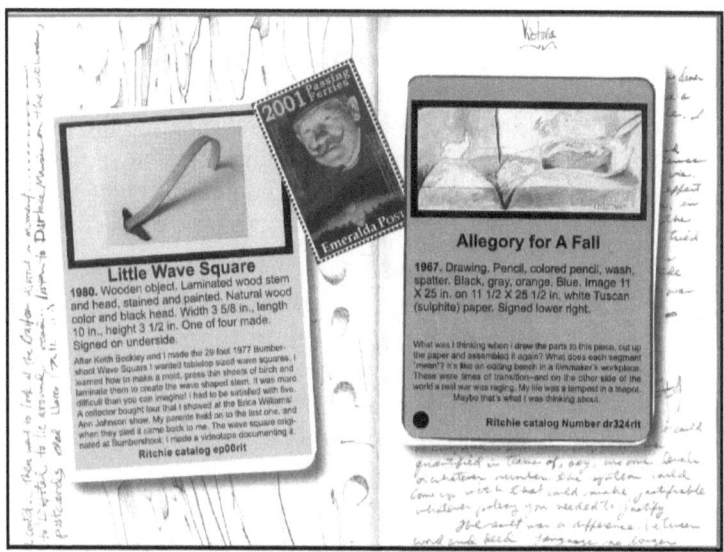

os980805
Automata in Emeralda Region
Demonstration in dumping the B.O.S.S. avatar

In her book Wellsprings of Knowledge, Dorothy Lambert-Barton recommends four automata, or avatars, to populate certain cells of Emeralda. Their wake-up call comes at the juncture of the river and lake in the author's visually inspired design of his games. 1104 Words.

os980815
What that professor said was boring
Launching a new phase of Emeralda

At breakfast at O'Studios, a cynical visitor records his thoughts as he is introduced to the concept development history of Emeralda. he is surprised to be (in a surreptitious incident) reading her story at the same time he is experiencing the next steps. 1476 Words.

os980825
So, you want to play Emeralda
Filling in your form

To fill out an application form to play Emeralda before the game is invented is premature, but during the inventing or testing of the game it's and exercise that can serve different purposes, giving valuable feedback to guide design by the user developer. 639 Words.

os980904
That old hyperlink feeling
Tracing a path back in time

Concurrently writing and inventing, the creator of Emeralda follows a thread so he can trace his own moves from his Score sheet model to the functions that each Cell may perform. In his imagination, an inspector questions him, police interrogation-style. 1641 Words.

os980914
Rewriting history
The SS United States, from America with Love

The male storyteller entertains himself every day with photograph that he takes of his daily routine. The snapshots it seem to him were his experiences in other times and places. This is the vision of th SS United States' conception and its restoration. 1045 Words.

os980924
Media family tree
Systems approach to Emeralda

Part XIII of Emeralda for Dummies. Drawing on a comparison with genealogy, the Emeralda newbie asks the question, "How do players get paid?" by looking at nature through the lens of the systems approach. Payment may come in forms of intellectual capital. 2322 Words.

os981004
Focus
Moving from focused individual to focus group

A cybernetic game starts with invention and then development-usually in that order. Between these stages is the focus group, which begins with a focused individual (the inventor) and continues to the focus group. This essay includes a sample E-mail Story. 1395 Words.

os981014
Q&A from O'Studios Agents
Emeralda Inventor Interviews

The Emeralda Inventor is visited by O'Studios Agents and they ask him questions about how Emeralda works, how he--the inventor--reconciles several dilemmas and paradoxes that seem to rise up out of his game theory--the theory of cooperation among players. 8722 Words.

os981024
Positively Curious About an Old Artist's Video
Why do I Have These Doubts?

The author reflected on a meeting he ducked out of that was partly to honor a 92-years old artist who enlisted him to help her distribute her videotape she made at 80. It was remarkable at the time, but now video is commonplace. How quickly people forget. 1092 Words.

os981123
Introduction to Emeralda O'Studios
The basics

Short-term goals are like ripples on the surface of water. Small regular intervals, they ride on the larger waves of long-term goals. Together they form a concert, creating a rhythm all their own. Its inventor thinks of Emeralda in terms of musical forms. 1592 Words.

os981203
Wealth in Emeralda E-mail
Watch those eggs

The Emeralda Inventor sees his daily e-mail as a special resource. He associates e-mail with wealth of mental and spiritual readiness to make wise choices. Watch the moments, as watching those moments is essential to human structural intellectual capital. 1800 Words.

os990107
Dream Time at O'Studios
Sharing a vivid memory

In Emeralda Region, the isle of the domains-of-expertise in hospitality includes storytelling and sharing of narratives in dreams, visions, flashes of insight and other entertaining and inspiring verbiage, pictures and performances. Following is a sample. 845 Words.

os990117
Critical Listening
Marketing creativity

The author was reading a memory expert's advice on improving memory and listening to the audio tapes that coached him through the expert's lessons. To make the learning more interesting to himself, he writes a narrative and applies it to his own history. 932 Words.

os990127
Multi Asking and Multi Answering
Conversing and scanning with the MFA

A fictional vignette by the creator of Emeralda and its islands, this one drawn from his role-playing in real life as a dental assistant's assistant or Multi-faceted Auxiliary. It's set on the fantasy island of O'Studios at lunch, and fun and games reign. 841 Words.

os990206
Will this be on the final?
Day one in the beginning course in Practice Management

The nightmare of finding yourself in class at finals testing time, and realizing it's your first day, may come true for the professor, too. From his 30-year old vision of a classroom of the future, the author describes a scene as if he sees it in a movie. 2034 Words.

os990216
Roots of DISCO-OP
A Story of and for Friends

The author paints in the background of DISCO-OP--also known as Dentalisco--and then develops a picture that shows how a cooperative approach came to be the core value upon which DISCO-OP is based. He tells how co-operation is the keyword to his successes. 2227 Words.

os990308
Speaking of Bad Days
A diary entry of an Apprentice User

In his diary of real-life and fantasy the Apprentice relates a remark about an impending doom. "Baby Boomers--numbering about 76 million souls of every race, credo and economic standing--have enough monetary wealth to destroy every living thing on Earth." 375 Words.

os990318
Artists Self- Esteem and Labor
Wisdom of investing in ability to labor

Self-esteem is not dependent on the physical products of work in studios. They will change because we change from minute to minute, bound to time and time changes everything. Artist's esteem is not dependent on the physical products of labor, but utility. 662 Words.

os990328
If Not for DVD It Does Not Exist
A flash of insight by an early adopter

A cryptic note foretelling the end of the trail for desktop computers and CD/ROMs that were of concern in the past of this artist/author's years. Now he says DVD is the end-all and be-all toward which his investments must be directed; nothing else counts. 296 Words.

os990407
Epiphany Economics
Your mortgage or your life

As if he's in the audience listening and watching a guest speaker (which is actually himself in role-play), the author relates how Epiphany is connected in his thinking to the mortgaging of your future and the connections to a general theory of economics. 1043 Words.

os990507
When Professor Bloom Plays Emeralda
Great Closings and Great Openings

Creating a new curriculum for on-line educational experience and relationships for knowledge workers requires research and what is called perfect information. In game theory, this means looking to the past for what is said happened and cannot be changed. 1255 Words.

os990517
The Multifaceted Auxiliary
New opportunities for knowledge workers

The Relationship and Experience Information Principle, or REIP, is the core of a new professional category called the MFA. The author is inspired by a guest editorial written by a dentist. As he role-plays as dental assistant, he opens gates to new ideas. 711 Words.

os990527
User's Groups
WIFM

User's Groups are like bridges over the chasm that separates IT industry's producers from consumers during their first generation. In its next generation, communication technology will likely re-live this bridge building, and re-frame the question, WIFM? 570 Words.

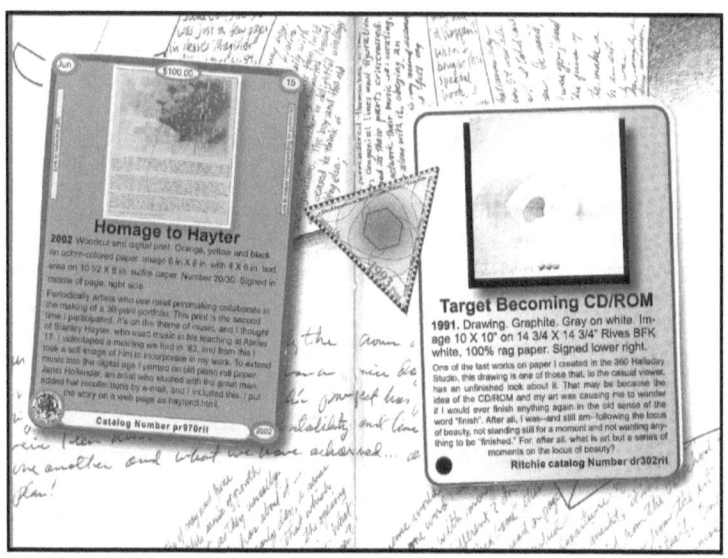

Homage to Hayter
2002 Woodcut and digital print. Orange, yellow and black on ochre-colored paper. Image 6 in X 8 in. with 4 X 6 in. text area on 10 1/2 X 8 in. suthla paper. Number 20/30. Signed in middle of page, right side.

Periodically artists who use relief printmaking collaborate in the making of a 30-point portfolio. This print is the second time I participated. It's on the theme of music, and I thought of Stanley Hayter, who used music in his teaching at Atelier 17. I videotaped a matching we had in '83, and from this I took a still image of him to incorporate in my work. To extend music into the digital age I printed on old piano roll paper. Janet Hollander, an artist who studied with the great man, added her recollections by e-mail, and I included this. I put the story on a web page as hayter01.html.

Catalog Number pr970rit
2002

Target Becoming CD/ROM
1991. Drawing. Graphite. Gray on white. Image 10 X 10" on 14 3/4 X 14 3/4" Rives BFK white, 100% rag paper. Signed lower right.

One of the last works on paper I created in the 360 Halladay Studio, this drawing is one of those that, to the casual viewer, has an unfinished look about it. That may be because the idea of the CD/ROM and my art was causing me to wonder if I would ever finish anything again in the old sense of the word "finish." After all, I was--and still am--following the focus of beauty, not standing still for a moment and not wanting anything to be "finished." For, after all, what is art but a series of moments on the locus of beauty?

Ritchie catalog Number dr302rit

---

os990626
Flight to O'Studios
A side trip survey

An imaginary flight over the Great Lake of Emeralda region serves to orient Emeralda's inventor to his next days of Resident Stay. Flying back over the island he just left he compares it to looking back over his personal history of prints and printmaking. 748 Words.

os990706
Look Back and Wonder
Where did we go wrong?

Owning an invention is like owning a huge lake--hard to control, hard to get your arms around. Like the elephant in the fable of the blind men, identifying it is part of the difficulty. The Inventor of Emeralda compares it to flying with a lost navigator. 622 Words

os990716
A Night at First Thursday
My opening at Sam's

He was an artist as he started careerism and, when he is bored, looking back at Perfect Information, the Inventor of Emeralda has a rich history in his design and craft of printmaking. An art opening is a perfect example of the entertainment at O'Studios. 595 Words.

os990726
The fundamental conundrum of HSIC
Least to own

To specify the action he wants his co-operative associates to take in his behalf, the inventor of Emeralda compares the background of his game to an artwork by the Dutch artist Mauritz Escher. "Drawing Hands" is a paradoxical work, rich with associations. 1007 Words.

os990805
Books and Poetry
Protecting the Gifts of Life

Four gifts of life--love, control, esteem and life itself--are protected from fear of losses by book, poetry and art. Dr. Viscott's speaking and books explain the bases for the rules of Emeralda, the Game for the Gifts of Life in this account of the game. 1673 Words.

os990815
Departures from O'Studios
Looking for the Pacific Digital Fine Arts Festival

Summertime in the Puget Sound--and in many states and countries around the world-it's time for arts festivals, crafts fairs and design displays. Most people in today's cultural centers enjoy them. But, the rest of the year, people can't attend-until now. 1026 Words.

os000107
Teaspoons and Tubfulls
Data data doo doo

Experiments in Art and Technology were BIG in the 70s. A veteran from those salad days reflects on his story as his path intersected those of art students of that era. He describes one who maintained his course, but not by experiments with new technology. 2057 Words.

os000117
The Last Artist Left
Please Turn Off the Lights

Role-playing as a student/provider in Art of Selling Art2 Online, a saleswoman makes her journal entry on a trip to a northwest US city,

Yakima, which she discovers has an amazing billboard. This suggests to her that Yakima might have a bad arts climate. 460 Words.

os000127
My Dinner with Jose
An Artist's Journal Entry

Short fictional journal entry from the life of an artist who is in an online course in business communications. She provides a vignette to demonstrate her ability to play Emeralda, the game that all the student/providers are required to use in the course. 603 Words.

os000206
Seven Hundred Words of Wisdom
The Prisoner Interrogated

A fantasy narrative or make-believe interrogation of the Inventor in his Emeralda Cell by a mysterious examiner who wants to know his plan for saving the Earth. The author is an artist with a vision that he follows in his practice of a game only he knows. 856 Words.

os000216
The Fastest Faux Painter
Taking care of business

An exercise in fast thinking for the fast artist, and, self-talking, he addresses himself to business planning. It's one he can share with another artist who says she wants to go back to the arts after a long absence from it. It's a brainstorming session. 595 Words.

os000226
So you want to be a sculptor in 2022
A letter to Old George

An ITinerate professor's letter to a prospective student as a dialog that he sees could happen over the Internet in a few years. It is a glimpse of an arts-based strategy intended as the Emeralda Inventor's proposal for an online K-K education curriculum. 385 Words.

os000307
Problems and Solutions
The Elmer Gates Prize for Online Art Ed

The problems that stand in the pathway the middle-aged and older people as they plan to fulfill their artistic, crafts person and designer visions are solved partly by solutions on the Internet. Specifying solutions is the job of the Emeralda inventor, an… 1205 Words.

os000317
Back to the Cascades
Springtime, 2000

Launch your own school and begin with the class of 2002. Prove you can teach online. Make partners. Let Emeralda Works be the software tester and a Web company. The secret to success is you know how to train sovereign individuals global quality standards. 593 Words.

os000327
Ticket to Ride
Two Generations Going Nowhere

The ITinerate professor makes outreach efforts to contact the people with whom he went to school. Few show interest in what he is interested in-higher education online, using the Internet to continue art education and the careers they once dreamed about. 465 Words.

os000406
Game Master Explaining Emeralda
The Master Speaks to Beginners

At the threshold of a new experience as role-playing a day in the life of the Emeralda Master, he tells the ongoing, inner dialog as a way of explaining Emeralda to ghosts in the new machine. In pauses between virtue and reality, he adds more definitions. 1566 Words.

os000416
Myartpatron.com Interview
Bill H. Ritchie, Jr, founder

An imaginary interview with himself (a favorite method of self-talking) helps his understanding of the branch of Emeralda Works that focuses on new ways to communicate with the art patrons. He considers it to be central and important in his artistic work. 1102 Words.

os000426
Everyone laughed when I sat down to write
Rear views are always funny

Want to know what the Emeralda Ball of 2022 would yield? A little rubbing and polishing, and here it is! In a room on the SSUS, the classmates are reminiscing-their 10th reunion. They recall when ProxiMates was new, a time when no one heard of Gary Tripp! 484 Words.

os000506
Geek Joke
Itinerate Professors are a laughing lot

He's trying out on-line auctions, thinking of ways to liquidate his life's work as an academic, maybe move on to other fields. He's caught by surprise when he gets a response about a houseful of theses and realizes it's only a typo. But it made him think. 755 Words.

os000516
Playing Proximates
Rules of the Game

Rule Number One is Do Not Procrastinate. Rule Number Two is Read Rule Number One. The Emeralda inventor seizes a day, as it is said, and the night, and casts his bid on the name of the game that will bring about another man's fame. A happy ending welcome. 205 Words.

os000526
MyProfessor.org
What is it?

The professor died. Long live MyProfessor.org! In his mission to teach and learn, research and develop by practice and production, this ITinerate Professor launches a new course-the realization of the concept that failed under the third university system. 417 Words.

os000605
Register now for the Gates Prize
You may already be a winner!

The lifetime of Elmer Gates is testimony to the importance of people being creative, inventive, discovering and imaginative. The Gates Prize awarded in his name to people who use contemporaneous technologies concurrently solving world problems is coming. 189 Words.

os000615
Calendars-Virtuous or virtual?
The Ghost and his Bride

Based on the popular motion picture, Ghost, and an obscure letter from a dead dentist to his wife, the author compares himself to the living dead in this story about the artist continuing to live in an after-life before life's end. He uses new creativity. 551 Words.

os000625
Happy Birthday, Mr. Gates
Nerds in the Archives

No sooner had the smoke from the birthday candles cleared when a boy appeared and without apology said, "Mr. Gates, I wish you'd come and see something." The birthday man looked around and smiled wanly, "Work calls . . .." Thus, begins a story installment. 1017 Words.

os000705
Mr Gates Meets Dr Osler
A Quick Look at What Might Have Happened a Hundred Years Ago

The author must have been daydreaming when he wrote this, but it is based on a sketchy outline about what might actually have happened between Elmer Gates and Dr. William Osler a hundred years ago. It is tongue-in-cheek humor by one who is on the pension. 744 Words.

os000715
Up in Smoke
In Memory of Paul Jenkins

A tiny flame licked the trailing edge of a wing. Who held the match also held a beer. I remember how she held that matchstick. It was poised delicately between her long index finger and thumb, and a diamond on the widowed finger, glinted in the firelight. 490 Words.

os000725
How myartpatron.com Got Its Start
Birth of a dotcom arts business

Developing a new branch of Emeralda Works requires exposing the basic idea. The creation of a so-called dotcom business is high-sounding and mysterious. This essay will explain there is no mystery but an ongoing tradition between artists and arts patrons. 1053 Words.

os000804
What Am I Good At?
Questions for My Art Patrons and Answers I Expect to Get

Raising capital for a new venture, the artist/author must face a test to see if he has what it takes to be a leader in the development of a business that sells specialized artists' tools. Before he can commit himself, he tests his ability to stay on task. 1232 Words.

os000814
What are you here for?
Four jailbirds tell their stories

In the personae of four imagined prisoners, the author portrays the four people he is thinking that play the leaders in the next phases of Emeralda Works' testing: As a drunken jazz musician, a cook, an artist and a teacher sharing their sad tale of woes. 2639 Words.

os000824
Woman Who Fell to Earth
An Artist's Story

Writing to the music of Mark Leonard's "Sheer Horizon", the Emeralda Inventor tries his hand at storytelling to establish the background tale for his role-playing game. Good games have stories to tell, and his is about four aliens from the Flower Planet. 2506 Words.

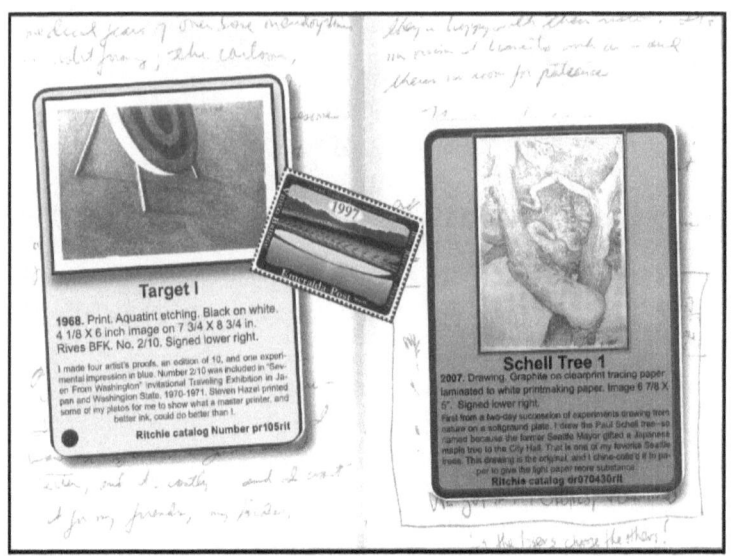

Target I

1968. Print. Aquatint etching. Black on white. 4 1/8 X 6 inch image on 7 3/4 X 8 3/4 in. Rives BFK. No. 2/10. Signed lower right.

I made four artist's proofs, an edition of 10, and one experimental impression in blue. Number 2/10 was included in "Seven From Washington" Invitational Traveling Exhibition in Japan and Washington State, 1970-1971. Steven Hazel printed some of my plates for me to show what a master printer, and better ink, could do better than I.

Ritchie catalog Number pr105rit

Schell Tree 1

2007. Drawing. Graphite on clearprint tracing paper laminated to white printmaking paper. Image 6 7/8 X 5". Signed lower right.

First from a two-day succession of experiments drawing trees native on a softground plate. I drew the Paul Schell Tree—so named because the former Seattle Mayor gifted a Japanese maple tree to the City Hall. That is one of my favorite Seattle trees. This drawing is the original, and I chine-collé'd it to paper to give the light paper more substance.

Ritchie catalog 9r070430rit

os001003
Revisiting Stamp World
Stamps and Stories and C. T. Chew

The author is a stamp artist, and discovered the stamp was also a subject dwelled on in a book about (and by) Charles Johnson-whose portrait is on a stamp. The words of its editor, Rudolph Byrd, were so appropriate that Bill appropriated and adopted them. 1502 Words.

os001112
Dusty and Trixie 1899
A short story for a Greeting Card

Bill and Lynda Ritchie have a secret. Each Christmas, they pretend to go back in time one hundred years and come up with an imaginary setting for their characters, Dusty and Trixie. This season they are living in Seattle, house-sitting, in the year 1900. 688 Words.

os001122
Dusty and Trixie on Holiday in 2000
A short story for a greeting card

Bill and Lynda Ritchie have a secret. Each Christmas, they pretend to go back in time one hundred years and come up with an imaginary setting for their characters, Dusty and Trixie. This season they are living in Seattle, house-sitting, in the year 1900. 851 Words.

os001202
Art Professor for Higher
Printmaking on A DVD - Part I

Potential text for a letter to introduce college faculty to a service or product the author is planning for release in May 2001 under the Living Prints label. It is a combination calendar and entertainment resource springing out of so-called edutainment. 787 Words.

os001228
Learning to Make Waves
A day in the life of an Emeralda Apprentice User

He would be the Pied Piper for the cruise-based course on art asset management and e-commerce on the Internet. Nine months before the cruise is to take place, the teacher is at work, honing his skills so he can stay at least one day ahead of the students. 1956 Words.

os010107
When Professors Run Away
Old Professors Don't Get Gassed, They Get Gassed Up!

Art Professor Ritchie "escaped" from the university ivory towers more than fifteen years ago, going from the fat into the fire. Now, after his long ordeal, a new opportunity is about to open up, thanks to the Internet. Ahead in creativity, he's doing DVD. 1105 Words.

os010117
Problems Aliens Face
Language Barriers

He pretends to be pleased that his passport passed the test that morning. When first he opened and submitted his to the Inspector at O'Studios, it failed. He's playing roles, so she suggested he take a position at a convenience system and seek his errors. 957 Words.

os010127
There Are VARs in the Stars
Why the art in other peoples' garbage out depends on garbage in

The author, an artist of the school of printmaking, observed his throwaway-become-artwork by a painter who later, became an art critic, turning garbage print into cash. By way of publishing he has a gift of horse's mouth as a value-added reseller, or VAR. 498 Words.

os010206
Image? You want Image?
I'll Give you Image!

The ITinerate Professor, with profound commitment to an image, a dream of a private art university online, responds to a comment by a renowned technology artist who said, "Nerds have no image," when he referred to the dilemma posed to artists by technology. 752 Words.

os010216
It was Bad in Toxi
In Between Got Worse

Artist turns cook to escape life in the city but finds himself a prisoner on a yacht. Instead of finding a new life he finds a kind of living death suspended between the worlds of virtue and reality, tradition and technology and production and livelihood. 1519 Words.

os010226
True Artists Don't Back Out, They Back Up
My 4-D Catalog In-Retro

Things that matter most to you should never be at the mercy of things that matter least, so the author remembers as he reflects on his former students in business and professions. These people are the complements to his half of his retrospective in art. 2118 Words.

os010308
Artist's Proposal for Alliance Marketing with Life Scientists
A Bigger Better Deal

After years of quiet research and development, the artist brings his plans to the tables of potential allies who want reformation of art and life sciences education using both sides of their collective experience. The author copy-writes a marketer's view. 1708 Words.

os010318
Artist's Proposal for Passing Ferries
Screen Play

Viva's VRAOB (Virtual Reality and Oxygen) Bar, first day of the year 2022. Evan, a tired-looking man about twenty--by his clothing and manner apparently a student--is taking a break from studies. Thus, begins a screenplay by role-player, Emeralda inventor. 440 Words.

os010328
How Do You Play Emeralda, Grandpa?
On the Prescience of a Three-year Old

The moment he reaches for a clean piece of paper to start the next chapter in his Emeralda Journal, the author imagines the voice of his granddaughter asking him how to play the game for the gifts of life. The answer touches on tetrahedrons paper folding. 821 Words.

os010417
Winning and Losing My Next Job
Short Happy Career and Future Search

Beginning with the End in Mind '92, the author began a new search at the end of his last real job in 1985. To tell about the end of that job would go a long way toward explaining the end of his Next Job, he says, at some indeterminable time in the future. 1979 Words.

os010427
Benefit the Artist in Residence
What's in IT for You (WIIFY)

What's in IT for an artist in residence who agrees to take part in the electronic age? As part of his K-6th grade strategic alliance design for EarthSafe 2022-his way of answering the UCS-the creator of this educational plan offers a list of the benefits. 440 Words.

os010517
Teaching Machines
Doing IT with Dusty

Art professor takes a new perspective on an old idea, getting out of his classroom to do some real teaching. Using new technologies to describe old methodologies, he starts with cave prints and ends up making DVD. He plots ElderVid, a series for MaturiTV. 1915 Words.

os010606
Why Play Emeralda?
So, you and your imagination can fly away

You and your creativity, inventiveness, discovering nature and imagination can get carried away when you play Emeralda, like getting carried away on an updraft in a glider, or away in an airplane. You can be the pilot, co-pilot and navigator for lifetime. 404 Words.

os010626
Amazing Amazon Art Supplies Online
What A Woman!

The author is a retired art professor, but you would not know it because he seems not to have actually retired. In fact, when you read this, you see he actually is a cast off from a sunken ship-art education. He proposes an art supplier with a difference. 3096 Words.

os010716
Tales and Details of A DVD Author
Counting and Accounting for the Future of Higher Education

A phantom voice asked this author, "What's important about those two letters, S & P?" and he was reminded that if a person is making one's own DVD, one must create a path that one can follow and a pathway one can trust. Others may follow, or they may not. 1670 Words.

os010726
The Ghost of Toulouse Lautrec in My New Machine
What shows change, what does not

A Virtual Assistant gives a guided tour to a long-dead but not forgotten painter, and visits the closet-studio of the Itinerant Professor of art. This professor writes concurrently, in free style, while his file is uploaded to the Internet theater nearby. 1265 Words.

os010805
Alert Artist's Teach Their Survivors
Teaching Wives to be Widows

First in a series that advise artists with ways to ensure the value of their legacy beyond their passing, saying that giving survivors the knowledge and skills for preserving the artist's lifeworks using new technologies is better than insurance policies. 1198 Words.

os010914
Basics of Art Education On-line Revealed
Art Professor explains his invention

The Itinerant art professor, inventor of on-line art education lists and explains four basics: The history of the university; the history of art schools and studios; the history of the rise of intelligent agents; the economics of triple entry bookkeeping. 1065 Words.

os010924
An Artist's Legacy of DVDs
Investigating A Missing Professor's Closet

A novel by a university professor about a missing university professor comes to mind as the author-and creator of a series of DVDs-counts how many DVDs he made. The fictional professor resembles the role-player the author invented, and lived, for himself. 909 Words.

os011004
Visiting Granny's DVD Workshop
Fancies of an inveterate printmaker

A way this writer creates essays is to copy down voices in his head (his grandmother's ghost?), imagining dialogs and scenes he wishes he really heard, alive. In this essay, he reports as a tour group visits his dream school, a printmaker/DVDmaker heaven. 1016 Words.

os011014
Stickers in Your Passport
Ten stamps and the way they fit history

A stamp artist who makes stamps for use in his Passports (for playing his game Emeralda) reflects on how his digital stamps are navigation instruments. He explains the terms of fine art and free fine art, and how a high school failed regional art history. 1417 Words.

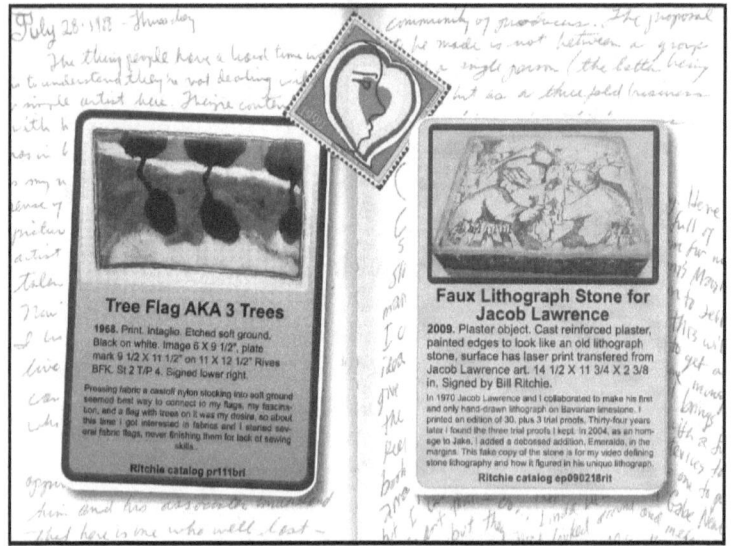

os011024
New Fundamental Art Education On-line Curriculum
How non-branded art serves a better vision

Driver education outsold art education says an art professor as he develops a fundamentally new form upon which to build an art education on-line curriculum. He thinks that 19th Century paradigms that dominated last century's art teaching no longer work. 1817 Words.

os011103
Thrill of Intercollegiate Arts
New dimensions in art education

Art education is about to burst out of the print era into the digital era of information and telecommunications. This will give a new dimension in which people who know a lot about the arts can work together on fresh new ideas for the benefit of everyone. 1548 Words.

os011113
D is for Disseminate
Reviewing the ICED Principle of Art Ed On-line

Gassing up for the road-it's an old notion behind disseminating ideologies today. But instead of cheap, petroleum-derived gas, this senior professor has taken a different road. He uses digital versatile discs to put his ideas out to worldwide audiences. 2338 Words.

os011123
Arts R Us
Art processes at a store near you

The wall between library users or art material suppliers' patrons and the artist's studio is removable by building an on-line database of art processes. Art educators need not teach everyone to be an artist, but they need to open windows on artists' ways. 1486 Words.

os020117
Writing Between the Paragraphs - Part 4
An imaginary dialog between two professors

An artist offers his perspective while reading the vision of Mark Taylor, professor of humanities. Taylor is one of the few who are viewing the place of arts in trends toward using more information and telecommunications technologies for higher education. 1116 Words.

os020127
No Teacher Left Behind
Closing the Art and Technology Gap

Passage of a bill in Congress may support arts education, and this writer sees opportunities in perilous times. He takes the first step, which is to match the bill with another real need, and names it: Teacher training for the age of digital reproduction. 1158 Words.

os020417
IT Works for Me
Asset Management and Legacy Transfer from an Art Professor's Viewpoint

The author takes the words Information Technology in the brief form, IT, and plays with phrases like IT works for me and IT works to put his arts and technology into perspective. Pictures, writing, databases and multimedia make his mediums for creativity. 379 Words.

os020427
Another Printmaking Panel is Born
Readying for the CAA Conference--again

Almost ten years ago the author made a presentation at the College Art Association meeting on the theme of Electronic Studios and the Artist as World Citizen. Another new opportunity is opening, but will he qualify? He studies the question like a student. 1815 Words.

os020507
Ethnography and Printmaking
Worlds apart, worlds alike on the Web and CD/ROM

The inventor of an interactive game intended for hybridized disc and Web distribution learned of a like-minded professor in ethnography who conceived a game for her students called Ethnoquest. His quest-like that of a field scholar-is likened to research. 633 Words.

os020517
Amenable Artist Interview
A sentient look at the artist, his art, computers and the Internet

He is asked if he would be amenable to being Interviewed, so this artist writes about his background and why he thinks nature's trees are like man's logic trees, an important basis for computer science and the arts. The story is not over, his essay warns. 883 Words.

os020527
A Tale of Two Towns
Prisoners Dilemma and the Web

An ITinerant professor strolls, wanders the Queen Anne Hill area of Seattle and finds, amid the parks and sidewalks of the artist's haven, a contest between business and the arts. He suggests playing the game out in John Nash style, in a Nash Equilibrium. 1244 Words.

os020626
Do Real Artists Write Business Plans?
Reflecting on the background of an artist/businessman

People think artists are one-dimensional, the result of generations of art education and promotion that worked in the postindustrial era of the last century. The age of digital reproduction changes this. This is a background of one artist's business plan. 1172 Words.

os020706
The Giant's Shoes
Caution-Visioneer At Work

On the edge of creating his life's dreams-his Perfect Studios-the multimedia artist is interrupted in his morning musings by an unexpected, ghostly guest. Over coffee he describes to his phantom guest how he plans to walk in the Giants' Shoes, his hero's. 1749 Words.

os020716
New Game Club in Town
Artistamps and E-Artistamps

What is the product of your business, they asked. Stamps, that is the easiest answer, and it may be the best. It may be the tipping point for Emeralda says the inventor as he prepares to meet the local Chamber of Commerce in the neighborhood of Uptown. 887 Words.

os020726
Stamp Uptown
Seeing the Neighborhood Through Stamps and Stories

The Seattle Space Needle stands for the old ways, Emeralda the new. In the author's vision, stamps and cards are in space like satellites spinning in the orbits of their makers. People use templates to get art-starts; he's got the Nitro to make it happen. 552 Words.

os020805
Artists' Games Building
Yesterday's, Today's and Tomorrow's Computer Games as Fun and Community

He left school at 43 to learn art's game, an artist and scholar's game he could take seriously for the remainder of his life. Occasionally he tells people how to play but it may not be communicable, like a player of solitaire before playing cards existed. 604 Words.

os020815
Investing in Labor, Not Silver Bullets
Not One Silver Bullet for Me!

Having acted locally for six months, the Itinerate Professor-enjoying the fruit of his labor on 2 years of his retrospective project-reaffirms the wisdom of investing in his abilities to labor in a changing marketplace for education, his best alternative. 662 Words.

os020825
How Mobile Devices Effect Education
Mapping and Microeconomics

Adding value to products of the digital age, such as portables, adds value to the teachers' assets because they do their best work when they move. Even on a short walk, they get better at teaching, research and practice, the keys for Itinerate Professors. 345 Words.

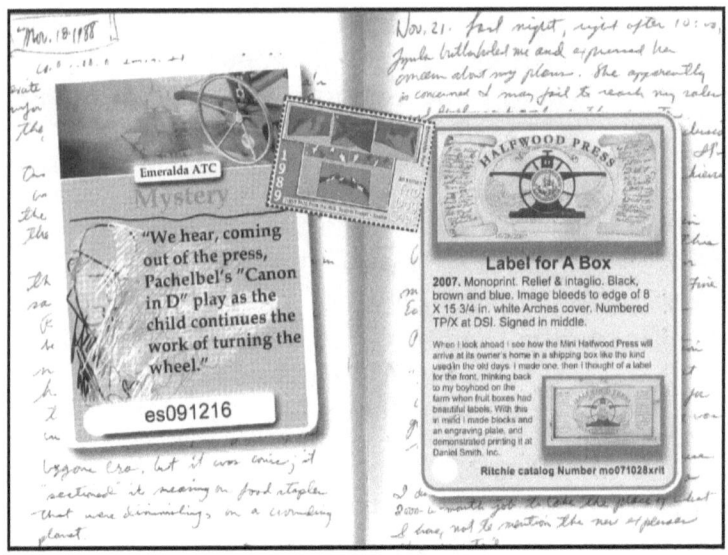

os020904
Connecting Four Dots
Art Festivals, Games, E-books and Artistamps

The 24/7 arts festival, Emeralda, a book titled the Artist's Last Love Letter and artistamps-are they connected like a dot drawing? They must be-and they all can play on DVD, this author's choice for his virtual, virtuous studio for this decade 2002-2010. 335 Words.

os020914
Mapping Artists' Routine Activity on the Web
Art Students Seeking Experts Look on the Net

Expert systems-one of the 20th Century engineering milestones-may now figure in art students' early careers in the 21st Century because information and communications allows them wider and deeper access to other learners, teachers, research and practices. 1180 Words.

os020924
Big Easy Education
Taking the Easy Way Out

A new paradigm for the future teacher is to take a harder path. To be effective is to skip the easy, site/event specific education models of the past. Distance education is tough but a lot easier if teacher/learners would be tough on themselves and do IT. 1246 Words.

os021004
Missing Professor's Closet Re-Opened
Another Paradigm for Art Ed On-line

Lines from another professor's book inspired this artist/professor-aspiring to be a virtual public intellectual-to reopen his metaphor of the "mystery of the missing professor's closet." He suggests his is the turnkey approach to an art education on-line. 1126 Words.

os021014
Visualize This
A WASHPIRG of Media Artists

His 1970s plan was a statewide multimedia center located in central Washington, but then an administrative coalition blockaded it. Thirty years later he's back, with a plan to empower the rightful owners of the dream-future Washington state media artists. 1589 Words.

os021024
Publish Electronically or Perish
Future teachers beware

A veteran of internecine battles in the US American professor power wars of the '80s describes how one has to experience death in the old system in order to survive and thrive in the future education field. He gives advice to young teachers on mobilizing. 674 Words.

os021103
Sighting O'Studios
Sense, nonsense and sight unseen

The Emeralda Defender is flexible but getting from one site to the next is demanding, almost ridiculously so because it is like nonsense. On the other hand, it's like Yoga in the morning-it wakes up my brain cells the way posing awakens up my enthusiasm. 451 Words.

os021123
Social Justice and Woodcuts
Challenging questions and a singing Barrista

Asked to support a new course in cross-disciplines, the artist/scholar organizes his thoughts to resonate with his social mission. The student's pre-digital structural contract challenges his plan to be more effective by using his new technology paradigm. 668 Words.

mr020825
File structure for stakeholders
Journal entry

The author describes the file structure for stakeholders. He describes how one is published annually and it is produced on a CD/Rom and a DVD. The chief value of the task is marketing in the spirit of "The Last Loveletter." 348 Words

os030117
Kite Story
Evolving a vision for animation

Sometimes a flash of an idea occurs, and you want to write it down, so you won't forget it. It might be the subject for an essay or a picture. With today's new animation software, it might be the concept for a movie-or, at least a flash. This describes one. 259 Words.

os030507
Imagine A Video Game
A Proposal for the Tacoma Art Museum

Possessing a private collection of early video art and experimental video-based work by regional artists, this author considers how he might liven up the collection with a digital game-based learning product. Could an art museum sell games in their store? 1400 Words.

os030527
We Build the Game as We Play It
How Stamps 'N Stories Got Its Start

Thinking ahead to a time when the game Stamps 'N Stories would be a big hit, the inventor/mentor considers the essential questions that he'll have to answer in order to achieve success. For example, who is the game for? Who is the market? Can anyone play? 1434 Words.

os030606
Saving for College
Two gateways

Billions of dollars are being put away for peoples' plans for college. Colleges are changing, however, and one wonders if people are really certain higher education is something which they think they're saving for. "Going to college" is becoming something else. 1530 Words.

os030626
Putting the S in TRPS
Service is where teaching, research and practice can take the virtual professor

The 21st Century artist is a game inventor and developer, working in the art form of the times, which is digital games. Although new, it's worthwhile to reflect on the past of art education in academe because the cornerstones of education haven't changed. 1180 Words.

os030706
Story of the Absent Professor
Background for an on-line art education digital-game based learning experiment

I have told the story of the absent professor several times until I'm beginning to believe it's the story behind my game, Emeralda: Stamps 'N Stories. It's about a teacher who never comes to class and how the students are better off because he planned it. 1581 Words.

os030716
I Get Letters
The emotional value of feedback

E-mail and snail mail are the heart of the Emeralda Stamps 'N Stories concept as the author reads a letter from a student to his professor in a distant state. His own e-mail carries value for him, and he wants to make this into a game that eases feedback. 1375 Words.

os030904
How to Create A Living Prints Online Hybrid Distance Learning for Profit School
Staying Alive in the Dying World of Fine Art Hand Printmaking

Taking his cue from an unlikely source (video games), the author connects the ideals expressed by today's visionary game developers with his own vision of a perfect teaching and learning online art studio that's focused on printmaking and multimedia arts. 1030 Words.

os030914
Fine Art Drawing in the Age of Digital Reproduction
A proposed book that needs and gets attention

He had a vision of a new school for art students suitable for their future-a future he could only say was a vision. Now the time seems to have arrived when such a school is close to reality and needs a textbook, so he starts with one of the basic classes.291 Words.

os031004
My Teaching Philosophy
Persistent State World Education

Reading the words of a persistent state world game developer is, to me, like reading my own worlds about how and why I teach. I could call it a philosophy of teaching. It's a philosophy that finds few homes in today's US American education scene, however. 1154 Words.

os031024
Have Tools, Will Travel
Bringing art ed into the 21st Century

What do a CD/ROM, a coffee shop and a laptop have in common? An itinerate professor of art (he's one who wanders around to teach, research, practice and serve) is considering these and how they're leading him to a new kind of online art studio experience. 1146 Words.

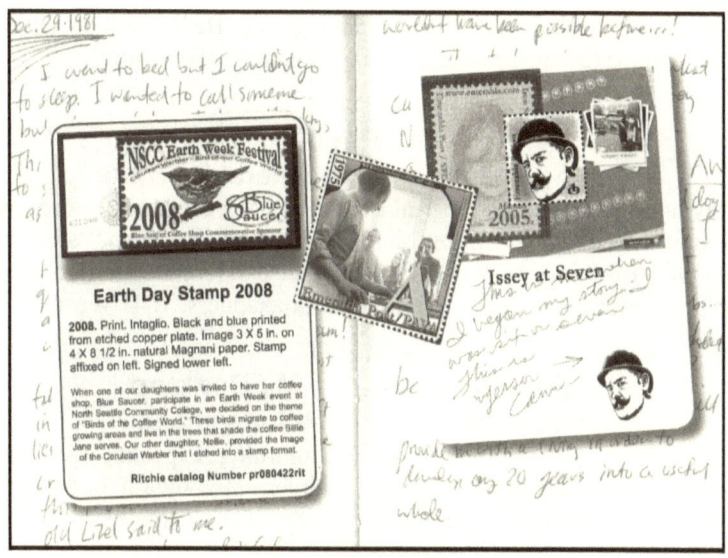

os031113
Dreams
What partnerships are made of
He's meeting with some of his former students, searching for a group to take the place of the virtual community he created in his game-like fantasy world. He's the "wizard" of Emeralda, and he's asking for a kind of formula to help artists save the world. 958 Words.

os031203
Visualizing My Studio
Starting all over again
When he resigned from teaching college 18 1/2 years ago his former student said, "Now you'll have to start all over like we did." But his vision was never the same as his students'-he was always ahead of the curve. Now he comes full circle, starting over. 845 Words.

os031218
Thinking About My Gallery
Towards a business plan
He's committing himself to opening an art gallery to showcase and sell his collection of art. This is not his first attempt and so he writes

about the venture in a business planning way. He'll focus on selling but continue production and developing games. 356 Words.

os031228
The Payoff
Getting Living Prints to Emeralda Works

Playing Emeralda has a magical quality because the inventor uses his computer to augment his intuition. By a chance encounter, using the search term Itinerate Professor, an obtuse reference to stochastic resonance turned up, leading him to rich metaphors. 1641 Words.

os040117
If Emeralda were on My Desktop
Getting the unexpected for a change

His habit of opening his e-mail every morning, expecting the same kinds of messages as he often gets, is interrupted by a new thought: What if he opened a game instead? What if the game he invented, Emeralda, were a substitute for the news he gets online? 1357 Words.

os040127
There is A Game in Me
Old songs in my heart, a paper in mind

He's searching for a reason for playing the game he himself invented in the 1990's and the answer hits him in the face while he's listening to music from the '60s and '70s-the era when he began to dream of a better world through being an artist and teacher. 450 Words.

os040206
One Day I Was Moving My Stamps Around
Pondering Emeralda, again

The inventor of a game he titled Emeralda reviews his collection of stamps that he made to commemorate his career in art, and as he does so he's inspired to think about making the game have an economic world of its own, drawing parallels with other games. 1338 Words.

os040226
When You're in Emeralda City
A vision of stamps for voyagers
You can look at over fifty artists stamps in the window of the gallery on Taylor Avenue in Emeralda City. When you choose one, you'll be transported-like magic-to one of the islands where the collection, of which that stamp is a part, is always maintained. 382 Words.

os040506
A New Journal Begins
Reflecting on Carl Sagan's Cosmos
Thinking a great deal about the attenuation of the printmaking division at the UW, where this author taught for 19 years, he relates Sagan's epilogue and Boorstin's account of the evolution of arts, architecture, opera and literature, culminating in film. 569 Words.

os040516
Filling the Printmaking Void
A proposal to replace the printmaking division at the UW
His whole life is devoted to media arts and education, and he's seen only one sustainable model for it: A University. Now that the university he knew is failing to sustain and grow the fine art version of the media arts, he offers the alternative: A Game. 1398 Words.

os040605
High School Printmaking on a Halfwood Press
A notion of a creative teacher
While in his studio early one morning putting wood strips on the edges of an etching press, a woman appeared at the door. Seeing a flash of color out of the corner of his eye while burnishing the wood was like Aladdin rubbing his lamp, and Demene came in. 808 Words.

os040705
My Character Flaw
Marketing the Mini Halfwood Press
The author has read a book on screenplay writing and learned that even the main character has a character flaw, even if cast in a heroic

role. Having finished a book on Ben Franklin-a printmaker like himself-he contemplates what his character flaw may be. 748 Words.

os040715
The Mini Halfwood Press at O'Studios
A tradition of printmaking going online

In graduate school he dreamed he would be a great teacher in the arts, specifically printmaking. He left the graduate school to go to teach at the University of Washington. Now he's dreaming of continuing to teach in a novel way using a tiny press for it. 590 Words.

os040725
Garden Parties, Dead Professors and the Mini Halfwood Press
Is there a connection?

A news article about a professor fighting for his name piques the memory of this "dead professor" who, actually alive and thriving, sees a bright future for such teachers as they can now, thanks to the Web, augment any discipline with a scope for fiction. 797 Words.

os040804
A Catalog in Me
Mini Press owners may publish plates

With the development of the Mini Halfwood Press underway, and as this opens the door to a new kind of experience in learning printmaking, the meaning of "having something in oneself" is changing for this artist/designer. This may come as a catalog in him. 569 Words.

os040814
Home and the Itinerate Professor
A miniature press is the key to mobility

What he has come to be (in the practice part of his art and craft) is the maker of a miniature intaglio printing press that allows the printmaking artist to move around. No longer anchored by a press, he-and people like him-can truly be "Itinerate" teachers. 1044 Words.

os040824
Changing Art Colleges
How outsiders will help bring needed changes
College art students don't realize it but art colleges have become like factories, and the students are the products. Students are raw material when they come in and finished products when they get out. Schools must change and help will come from outside. 511 Words.

os040903
Share A Legacy
Funeral Notices in the Times
As he ponders the next stage of his work as an Itinerate Professor in an age of digital reproduction, he notices an ad in the Seattle Times for a legacy-saving proposal in their obituary section. It compares nicely with his dream of online legacy transfer. 1134 Words.

os040913
Emeralda Reminder
The importance of file structure
He invents a game he calls Emeralda: Games for the Gifts of Life but after 12 years he's still not sure how to explain it. Playing it is all he lives for, since it's based on his lifework of education and arts. A chance encounter reminds him how to start. 805 Words.

os040923
Interview of a Future Art History Major
Testing a theory
Halfway through the transcription of a videotape he's preparing for an archive, the author is interrupted. Outside himself, looking in, he wonders how that which he's doing would look to some stranger. Role-play is sometimes a good exercise, so he starts. 1660 Words.

os041003
On Broken Links
The Importance of being consistent
An email from a Net surfing doctor tells him two links are broken on his Elmer Gates site. After thanking the doctor and repairing the links, the author reflects on the importance of long-term consistency and how a daily routine of database updates helps. 553 Words.

os040824
Daniel Opens the Professor's Archive
Dreams to become a teacher are coming true

A man named Daniel wrote in a listserve that he wanted to finish his college degree. He would like to do this online if such a program exists, and he asked. This author, reading his request, visualizes some links between online higher education and games. 840 Words.

os041023
Losing My Grip
Between a hard place and a soft place

The author has spent many years considering the software that has grown up around him and his devotion to education-too many years perhaps. Now he's got a hand on a piece of hardware, and an opportunity to make art instruments. It poses a dilemma for him. 888 Words.

os041102
My Autobiography at Open Studios
A better way to write your memoirs

He has a friend who wrote her autobiography in her 'nineties, and he thinks that it's better to start early, not waiting for a publisher to join the task. Also, it's better to spread the project over many domains and lastly it's better to use cybernetics. 803 Words.

os041203
What is the Moment?
From found object to game play

A casual remark by an acquaintance stirs renewed interest in a part of the game, Emeralda called moments. "You are so in the moment," his friend said, and she proceeded to compare the artist to a girl child she knows who, when walking, always finds money. 886 Words.

os041218
Five Little Presses All in a Row
Mini Halfwood Presses where my plates ought to be

It seems like a turning point in his career as the author eyes five tiny etching presses sitting in his studio. On the walls are the products of the first forty years of his career in the arts. The presses may mean that these are the last artworks he created. 788 Words.

os041228
Imagining Students
The missing professor dreaming
Twenty years ago, he was set adrift from the flagship university, left to navigate the waters of the real world alone. Today he's come upon a new land, like a castaway on to an island and his navigation skill makes him a new artist, designer and craftsman. 568 Words.

os050107
Becoming A Craftsman
Turning Point in the Artist's Road
He's spending much more time on craft than he spends on art. And what he's crafting he designed. The old professor of art contemplates what it means to have advocated "art, craft and design" his whole life while he works on a small handmade etching press. 623 Words.

os050117
Things That Matter Most
Must Never Be at the Mercy of Things that Matter Least
The phrase, Things that matter most must never be at the mercy of things that matter least, lies at his consciousness as he surveys the tasks before him. But how do you decide what's important and what's not important? He thinks his game will help decide. 836 Words.

os050127
Emeralda Habits
Be Proactive
Be Proactive, begin with the end in mind. 52 Words.

os050206
Returning to Work
Lifelong lessons from someone who's been there
The retirement fund that pays him his monthly annuity asked for ideas on returning to work and lifelong learning. This writer's experience is too unique to be much value, but he tries his hand at responding, anyway. "Invest in labor," he quotes an expert. 1280 Words

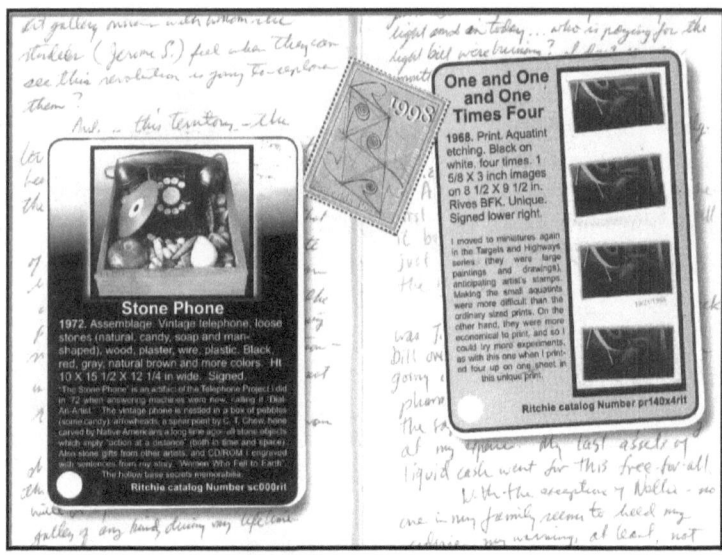

os050216
Third Life in Emeralda Land
Comparing Emeralda with Second Life

There's food for thought and work for the brain in a comparison of a video game called Second Life and the game this writer envisions that he calls Emeralda. He focuses on intellectual property rights, or intellectual capital, as the payoff in both games. 632 Words.

os050226
Emeralda-The TV Show
Glimpse of the Future

The author, who claims to have invented a game he calls Emeralda: Games for the Gifts of Life, frequently meets challenges from well-meaning friends and former students, telling him to explain his game. Until he thought of a TV show, it seemed impossible. 935 Words.

os050308
Like Opening A Deck of Cards
Early Morning in Emeralda Play

He thinks he'll play a game he invented for the rest of his life if the subtext of the game means anything. Games for the Gifts of Life means using one's talents and cultivating them so that they benefit oneself and one's community as long as one lives. 612 Words.

os050318
Starting A New Career
Using the Gifts of Life

Upon reflection, the author/artist realizes the new career he's launching is one of the gifts of life he has written and visualized in his daily routine. Of late he has searched for the meaning of his game, Emeralda, and his making of the miniature press. 534 Words.

os050328
Emeralda's Big Payoff
Multitasking and Age Resistance

Two articles he read about children and oldsters has this artist/writer excited. One says most children multitask with media technologies, the other says using one's whole brain wards off the decrepitude of an aging mind. The payoff is in game strategies. 1560 Words.

os050407
Using Kwanzaa
Community Virtues and Storytelling

A book about Kwanzaa, the African American celebration of the gifts of life, inspires this author/artist to find parallels with his own way of celebrating "gifts of life". He finds the teacher's story holds valuable lessons that she learned from children. 736 Words.

os050417
A Way to Publish Plates
An Idea Worth Testing

He's been wondering how to publish plates that go with the Halfwood Presses, items that will help people learn more about printmaking and doing this by using the Internet. Now he thinks he's got a key idea, and that is to publish the images for downloads. 595 Words

os050427
Love and Banishment
Excerpt from Vladimir's story

Vladimir was forbidden to leave his island by the native, first Nation people. The reasons are complicated, having to do with the island as being a sacred place, and the white explorers' violations. He was held in favor and curiosity, however, partly bec… 295 Words.

os050507
A Curious Find
Grounds for the Yarn of the Emeralda

As part of his marketing plan for a small printing press that he designed, the author wrote a story about an 18th Century mystery ship that sank and had a printing press aboard. This notion seemed far-fetched until he discovered a similar tale in a novel. 1303 Words.

os050517
Emeralda Year
A Year of Living Copiously

Robert Grudin is a writer (Book: A Novel) and professor who contributed to the development of the game Emeralda: Games for the Gifts of Life—without knowing it. Examples are his illumination of the copious, and new way of calculating the length of a year. 1146 Words.

os050606
It's in the Cards
Telling Your Story in Emeralda Artist Trading Cards

Stephen Covey, the renowned author, said, "The deepest hunger of the human soul is to be understood." Emeralda Artist Trading Cards, in the Games for the Gifts of Life, may be one means by which people can tell their stories in a creative, reflective way. 546 Words.

os050616
Artist Finds Himself Living in His Own Game
Castaway Art Professor Role Plays his Way Back to Life in the Age of Digital Reproduction

There's something about a headline catches his eye, and this artist—who also likes to write—finds his own life to be like that of the renowned author, Terry McMillan. Few think so, nonetheless he deconstructs her story and learns more about his dilemma tale. 978 Words.

os050626
The Story of Vladimir Petroslovena Chichinoff
A Story about A Cabin Boy

This artist works with brass and copper sheets about the size of playing cards, etching an image of a map of an imaginary place that he calls Emeralda Region. How such an image came about is a long story and begins with a Russian boy who was lost at sea. 5000 Words.

os050706
Teaching Emeralda
First Lesson Plan in Emeralda 'Zinemaking

He has invented a kind of game to play as one's years reach beyond fifty into an unknown future. This game is like Solitaire, played with cards, or, sometimes, with stamps, but always with creativity, invention, discovery and imagination. Can he teach it? 476 Words.

os050716
I Dreamed I was in My Own Archive
Taking the Task

Wanted: RA to review the archives of former professor of art. Archives consist mostly of digital material. Candidate must be a good reader, detail oriented and skillful with software for text, graphics and multimedia. Writing skills a plus. 291 Words.

os050726
A Script for Laser Print Etching
Getting Ready for the Big One

This printmaker (he's one who loves to teach people his "secrets") gets ready for what might be his most challenging of his one-hour demonstrations: Laser Print Etching. He must use tricks to speed up the process for his audience, so he scripts his steps. 690 Words.

os050805
Putting the Press Before the Horse
Reflecting on Public Versus Private Teaching

A comment that he wrote in his journal a year ago sets the artist probing the meaning of teaching in the public eye compared to private teaching and confirms that it is necessary for printmaking students to learn the importance of owning their own press. 906 Words.

os050815
A Grant for Education
Connecting A Game with Startup Money

He is encouraged to find a grant writer to develop a game he calls Emeralda: Games for the Gifts of Life. Defining the game has been a slippery process—the form of the game changing with the seasons and his mood. Is this a way to approach a grant proposal? 508 Words.

os050825
Online Art Learning Boom
Seattle's Emeralda Academy

Copy-writing over an article by Linda Shaw, a Seattle Times staff reporter, the artist and former professor envisions what she described as applied to arts taught online. He uses the original article about the online learning boom to reinforce his vision. 1768 Words.

os050904
Trading Cards for Education
An Online Art Course in My Incubator

Simply because trading cards were meant for fun doesn't mean they can't teach something. This author, in his sixties, can still remember how collectible cards influenced his education. He thinks that if commercially made cards can teach, so can originals. 578 Words.

os050914
The Successful Communaire
Considering the Way of Practitioner Communities

His long-term vision for a working and living community is modeled on his lifelong experience with practitioner groups of all kinds, from schools to condominiums. He writes down what he thinks make him qualified to participate in a new artistic community. 1095 Words.

os050924
Fast Forward to 2008
Vision of Little Prints—Again

In his mind's eye he sees a day like today—at Open Studios & Hospitality—taking place in a gallery he named Little Prints. It is a place focused on miniature prints and the miniature presses on which they're produced. It's a kind of learning gallery, too. 574 Words.

os051004
A Stamp 'N Story A Day Keeps My Brain Alive
Thought on Past and Future Artists Stamps

He's planning a demonstration in the making of artists stamps into gifts and considers for a while the role that artists stamps play in his daily life. He created a calendar on his computer and placing stamps into it is like filling an album of his life. 528 Words.

os051014
Food Stamps and Artist's Stamps
An Approach to Online Printmaking Education

Browsing a local newspaper one day this artist gets a quick introduction to recipes online. It's strange, because he's really interested in ways to teach printmaking using computers and his MiniBooks and Mini Press. He suggests stamps and food are linked. 1087 Words.

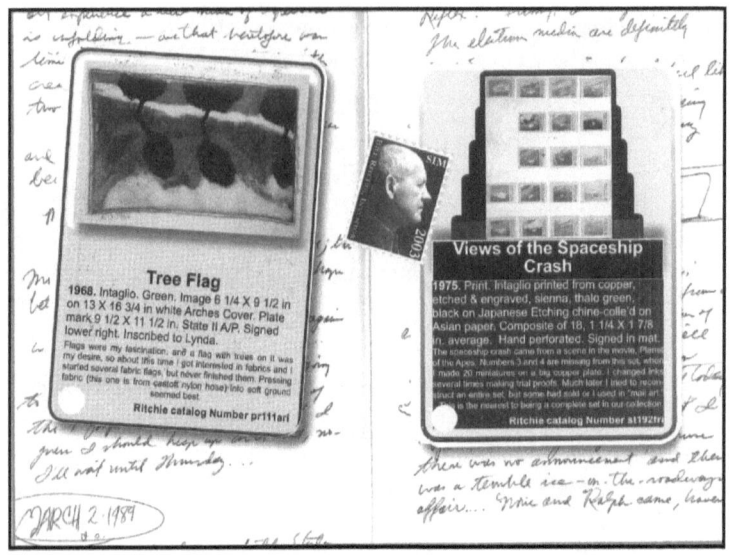

os051024
Total Proof for Printmaking Benefits
Art and Craft of Etching is Good for Students

Hands on crafts projects are good for kids' education. This essay is the response to reading a report by a hobby industry journal that says kids do better at reading and other academic skills, plus social skills, when hands on projects are part of school. 2100 Words.

os051103
Where Should We Be Today?
Reflections on Three Generations of Art Students

What would his curriculum look like today if he hadn't been forced to resign twenty years ago? That is what's on the mind of this former art professor as he has on an online dialog with a former student. In this essay he speculates on what could still be. 1098 Words.

os051113
Imagine A Cable Head Art Store
Fast Forward to 2008

He's fantasizing about an art store that actually was a transmission point for short demonstrations of art techniques—sort of a Martha

Stewart of the art, craft and design field. As an artist and teacher, he has long wanted to reach people beyond schools. 503 Words.

os051123
Making Artist's Stamps Count
Going Beyond the Look of Political Art

Approached by a gallery director to get involved in an exhibit of art on political themes, this artist—making artists stamps—realizes he never made a work of art with a political theme. He says that artists stamps may be political but by different design. 1053 Words.

os051203
Secret of the Emeralda
Discovery of the Oceanographer's Sea Chest

How can you share secrets of days gone by? Does anyone really care about a printmaker's secrets or is this just another blind alley that the creative person must explore? This is the newest challenge facing the inventor of a game that only he knows about. 1182 Words.

os051218
How I Use Computers in My Art and Craft
Let Me Count the Ways

This artist and craftsman has been wanting to teach people how to use their computers in the arts and crafts. He believes most teaching on this subject misses the mark, for others treat the instrument as though it were merely a tool. 792 Words.

os051228
Authors and Artists
A Card Game Metaphor

Inspired by a description of an old card game titled Authors, this artist considers whether it could serve as the metaphor for a card game involving artist's stamps and stories in the context of a digital game-based learning experience. He tries his hand. 826 Words.

os060107
Smart Condos
A Game-Frame of Living

Because he lives in a condo (where he never thought artists should abide) and partly because he thinks artists should be community-living activists this artist is dogged by awareness that his interest in game theory and practice is stuff for a condo game. 1010 Words.

os060117
A Bigger Splash
Imagining A Bigger Halfwood Press

Should his current project—making small and beautiful, functioning etching presses—turn into a bigger company and not remain a one-man show? This artist ponders the question in light of his perspective on the age of digital reproduction and art education. 473 Words.

os060407
Secret Lives of Sarah
Lives touched by Sarah Spurgeon (1903 - 1985)

An artist whose life was touched in many ways by his art professors' teachings and exemplary personalities sets about the creation of a CD/ROM that he thinks will contribute significantly to the art gallery of his Alma Mater—Central Washington University. 431 Words.

os060417
Over My Shoulder
Sarah's ghost and my new machine

This artist, a former student of a well-liked teacher, ponders the question, "What would she say if she could see me now—moving digital files around on my computer hard drive?" He concludes, considering the times she probably would not know what to think. 1236 Words.

os060427
Three Students
Brainstorming for the Virtually Sarah game idea

This artist says games are the art of the 21st Century and he'd love to go back to college and advise his professors so they could change ways of preparing their students. The problem is that most of them are dead. So, he imagines himself as starting over. 1177 Words.

os060507
Senior Game Design
Imagine a virtual seminar

The author, a former student of Sarah Spurgeon (his old professor, after whom the college art gallery is named and now needs supporting money) pretends he is enrolled in an online course in digital game-based learning, and he has been given an assignment. 221 Words.

os060517
Community Key
Printmaking as a shared art

Divorced from its ties to painting, drawing and sculpture, while honoring those arts, printmaking comes closer to an art of community-building through sharing ideas, images and experiences. An important role in society develops when prints become digital. 383 Words.

os060527
Play quip for Sarah's Ghost
Notes from a dreamer's journal

In 2006 he had an idea for a fundraiser to help improve the Sarah Spurgeon Art Gallery at Central Washington University – where he had gone to school in the 1960's and studied with her. The play was to be "Sarah's Ghost," unfortunately it never got suppo... 196 Words.

os060716
Auction and Reflection
More than A Database

His art auction is once again removed from traditional auctions and eBay, yet his auction draws certain elements from these. The intent is not only to make sales and raise money, it's also an artistic device. 396 Words.

os060726
Ticket Art
It's Different

The images on the ticket are of the artworks that will be in the auction/play. It's an idea nurtured during the vast plan to help his alma mater and the Sarah Spurgeon art gallery in the Reino Randall art building – a vast idea with a half-fast plan. 230 Words.

os060805
Reframing Printmaking
Two Overlapping Frames

The author constructed a different importance for art. You might say he saw art through two overlapping frames: One was its role in society and the other was its role for the creative, sovereign individual. 1322 Words.

os060825
A Place to Study This
The Search for A Center for Study of Video Game Based Art Education

After a generation of teaching in a traditional college art department, this author left the campus to extend what he had learned about the basics of using technology in art and the teaching of art processes. His goal is to become a virtual art professor. 1433 Words.

os060904
Game Purpose and Narrative Purpose
How Emeralda Works

Emeralda is a game for learning media arts in a group, as in a cooperative game. It also has the flavor of a treasure hunt. You might compare it to the game Clue. 1150 Words.

os060914
Blogging Art
Games for the Gifts of Life

The Internet, and things like blogs, wiki spaces and Web sites have given writers another voice. Not only do these offer hope of distribution of writers' ideas, they also give other creative people hope. 550 Words.

os061004
Fragging Students
Clippings for Student Journals

Every week the students receive something to paste into their journals. Sometimes it is a story, printed so small it takes very good eyes, or a magnifying glass, to read it. Usually the students reformat it into larger type to make it readable. 317 Words.

os061024
What Does the Bible Contain?
Game Development

Every game has what is called in the gaming industry a "bible." The game's bible contains everything there is to know about it, from the game's inception onward. 450 Words.

os061103
You Will Make A Hyperlink
Putting Excel Spreadsheets to Work

A hyperlink is your exit from the Excel spreadsheet that accounts for your Year of Living Copiously. That is your Gates Prize. Remember that the Gates Prize is awarded before you earned it. 656 Words.

os070107
Harris is your character in Emeralda
Comparative investing

The man who would be the game inventor for Emeralda: Games for the gifts of life, reflects on national economics, incorporating his personal economics and Emeralda, brainchild for artist's asset management and legacy transfer compared to capital investing. 725 Words.

os070606
History of the Halfwood Press Ch 8
Open Studios and Hospitality - 8th Day

A day at the Taylor Avenue Studio, a viewpoint from a visitor in June. 2420 Words.

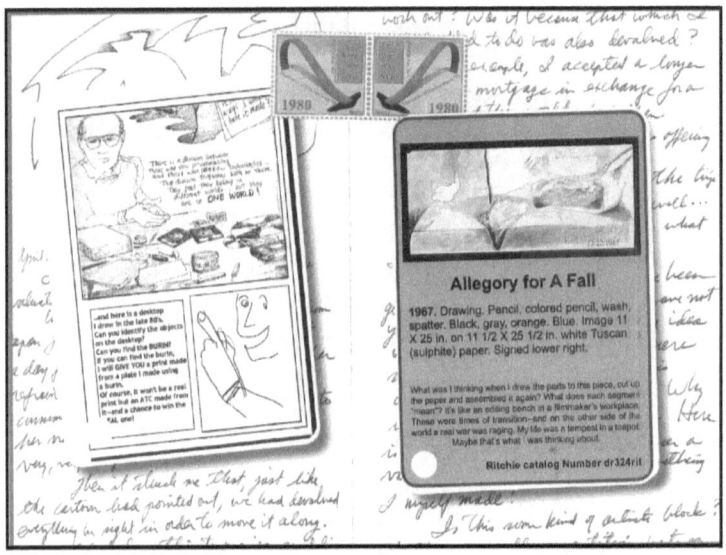

070626
Notes for instrumentation performance
Back story of a printmaking and music show

Paul Pauper, an artrepreneur who had been given a show space in downtown Seattle, contacted the author and arranged a show where he wanted to host a performance work alongside the artworks on the wall. These notes provide a back story and a press release. 770 Words.

os070928
Plate Story
Magic in the Metal

This printmaker comments on hearing voices while wiping his plates to print. He is an etcher, and he uses copper plates. This makes him think there's magic in the metal and, like the bottle that contained a Genie, when rubbed, frees his storytelling muse. 678 Words.

os071014
First Play
Emeralda Card Game

The development of the idea and the process of playing the game he calls "Emeralda" required an attempt at play testing. His wife joins him for this run-through, and he wrote the process down as they played it. 524 Words.

os071024
Lifelong Employment
Dividends and Prizes for Participants

Participants earn dividends and win prizes for their skills. A central piece is the press itself. The emphasis is on intaglio and relief printmaking, and possibly stencil. 230 Words.

os071103
Deck of Ten
Emeralda's Collectible Artist's Trading Cards

While he is in the grips of creating lookup tables for the twelve years when he received the Gates prize and, in the pattern, emerges an answer to a basic question regarding the cards: How many cards come in a deck of Emeralda Collectible Artist's Trading Cards? 501 Words.

os071203
New Game
Owning and Selling Artwork within A Game

One player, the owner, presents an object for sale. The owner speculates it is worth $100+ and will allocate a percentage to a game master when it is sold. The master may ask for any percentage, knowing the proceeds will be shared with other players. 571 Words.

os071218
Merkin Dilemma
Making Sense of a Trading Proposition

An art collector says he's joking—that he's a joker—when the Emeralda inventor reads his email and sees the proposal to trade one of his artworks for that of a former student and makes a counter proposal to trade an artist's trading card about the artwork. 742 Words.

os071228
Blank Card
Emeralda's Intangible Gifts

Emeralda is about intangible gifts. The author saw the art world from a different point of view, it is only in the age of digital reproduction that Emeralda could exist. This point of view could not exist without his knowledge of video art and computers. 586 Words.

os080107
Complete Works Game
Considering A Traditional Publication

Cleaning off his desktop one day he finds part of a sheet of uncut artist's stamps—his own—under the clutter and, curious, he discovers he had left off on a project of creating an illustrated catalog of all his works. Could it be published cheaply today? 777 Words.

os080117
Solitary Play
A Form Game to Create Time

Why do people play alone, as in the game Solitaire? This form of game is based on chance and scarcity, where you seldom win. In another form of solitary play, the author explores a game that is based on chance and plentitude, the artifacts of a rich life. 980 Words.

os080127
Flash Cards
A New Auction Idea

Instead of a catalog, visitors have decks of cards consisting of the works to be sold at auction. 88 Words.

os080206
Serious Games
Spurious Curious Regional Game Inventor

There are many serious games you can read about and even buy on the Web. Which, if any of them, have meaning to you? If you find there are none because they are based in professional and educational fields, then you have an opportunity to invent your own. 1023 Words.

os080216
Legend Making
Three Works in One

A happenstance usage of the word legend starts this print maker (also a maker of printing presses) in contemplation of the meaning of the word as it applies both to the interpretation of maps and storytelling. He thus wonders if he might be three people. 711 Words.

os080226
Today's Game
Better to Invent A Game than Do Nothing at All

It is said that Confucius advised, "Better to play games than do nothing at all." This artist calculates that it is even better to invent a game than anything else, and help other people play it. So, daily he thinks of a game to play with art. 401 Words.

os080327
Contrast/Complement
Principles of Two Ages

In the age of mechanical reproduction, black contrasts with white; blue complementary to orange. In the age of digital reproduction, contrast and complements in the making/playing of the collectible artist trading card version of Emeralda. 844 Words.

os080426
Big Mistake
Dean's Advisory Council

Hoping to find the perfect community of practice through the Dean's gateway, going to a reception for the Dean's Advisory Council was a Big Mistake. 590 Words.

os080506
First Review
One of Three

Soon he will be in a world of his course, Learn Printmaking Online, and he must consider the nature of the new course against the conventions of teaching he once practiced in the old, dying world of printmaking. There will be reviews and preparations. 1088 Words.

os080516
Faculty Support
First of the Twelve Tasks
Faculty Support, as the ninth of the twelve tasks of the successful manager of Learning Printmaking Online (or, as Professor Beaudoin wrote it out completely, training and support for faculty) needs to be at the top of the list. 1023 Words.

os080526
Data Definition
A Parable about Muses
Four women who fell to earth are with the author much of his waking time, and they coach him. But each of them has a unique coaching style. 1133 Words.

os080605
Functioning Enterprise Organization
A Whisper from Media
Tell someone in Australia and someone in Chile they are playing a game called Emeralda that is about Learning Printmaking Online. To play, they must have a Halfwood Press. 743 Words.

os080615
Business Plan
The Motivation Column
In John Zachman's chart titled "Enterprise Architecture – A Framework™" there is a Cell G3 that is labeled Business Plan, Where End equals the Business Objective and the Means equals the Business Strategy. 648 Words.

os080625
The Work of Art in the Age of Digital Reproduction
A Textbook for Learning Printmaking Online
The Open University concept suggested teachers could adopt the methods of commercial communication—mail, telephone, TV, etc.—to reach their students. 412 Words.

os080705
Detailed Representations (Out-of-Context)
The Sub Contractor Role

In Zach Man!, one of the objectives is to invest in labor, as directed by Paul Hurd in the book, The Retirement Myth, by Craig Karpel. 269 Words.

os080715
Would You Buy This University for Your Grandchild?
A Game for Finding Universities or Collages

At a private dinner on July 4, 2008, the author was given a challenge: What kind of game would help foreign students pick an American University or College? 899 Words.

os080725
Job Description
Team for Owner Support and Benefit Development

The job initiated by Nellie Sunderland, our daughter, entails database management and improvement. 385 Words.

os080804
Aim of the Game
Towards A Ninety-day Wonder

The professor meets a game designer who is fluent in new methods and they agree to win a contest using a tool called Silverlight, sponsored by Microsoft and ending on October 31. They plan to use the contest victory as a benchmark in the game development. 233 Words.

os080814
Professor Introduces Printing Game
An Imaginary News Article

Wondering how he can convey the nature of his project he calls Learn Printmaking Online to many people; he thinks a news article would be suitable. But who would write it? In the fashion of one who enjoys a vision of the future, he tries to write his own. 678 Words.

os080824
La Quatro Angelos de Emeralda
Writing in Spanish

Why does the author write the title in Spanish? The Four Angels of the Emeralda is a story he can write in English much faster! Perhaps he wants to slow down. That way every word can be considered more carefully. 1121 Words.

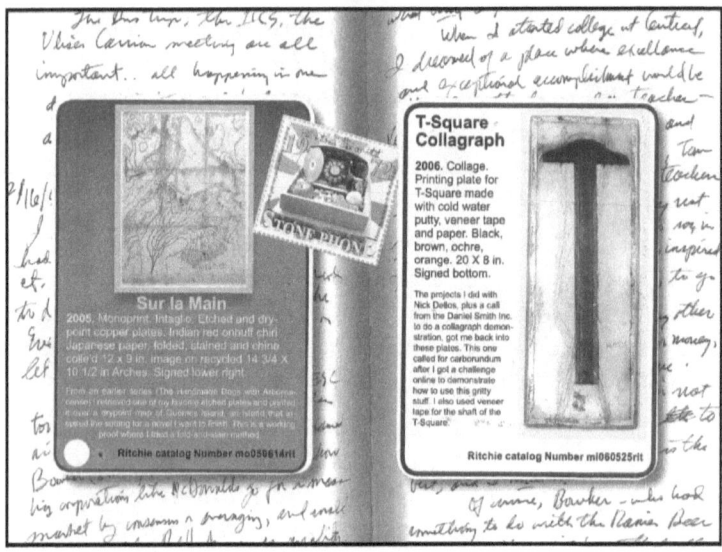

os080903
Requirements
Art Student Accountability in the Age of Digital Reproduction

Students must fill their passports to pass the course. Stamps from each domain-of-expertise must be cancelled by the professor and his cohort. Stamps must be accompanied by a story. 212 Words.

os080913
To Die For
What to Do Before I Die

For the author, a thing to die for is achievement of his lifetime goal, which is to be known as a great teacher. 468 Words.

os080923
Ten Years of Small Is Beautiful
Year One is ArtsPort

He begins, "When I was in Kansas …" It's a "theme" for an art exhibit based on the islands in Emeralda. 170 Words.

os081003
The Best Thing about Baldwin City
Reflections on Baldwin City

After ten presentations, the professor is asked what his favorite thing about his residency was. He's at a loss but concludes that it was that the visit to the small liberal arts Kansas campus kick-started his imaginings for future projects. 837 Words.

os081013
Be A Part of the Coming Revolution in Printmaking
Bill Ritchie's Invitation to A New Community of Practice

The author claims forty-five years of being a printmaker, and these generations showed to him that an evolution has been underway during that time. Now he claims a new printmaking world is on the horizon and he wants to invite people to participate in it. 806 Words.

os081023
Plotline for Amina
Where Does She Go from Here?

Writing for a video game is not like writing a story or a screen play. Reading has told this author that fact, yet it is not clear just how to do it. It's straightforward to write for video cut scenes, but a game is interactive, which challenges a newbie. 552 Words.

os081102
Professor Magee's Message to Amina
An Example of Transfer

From reading What Video Games Have to Teach us About Learning and Literacy, the artist/teacher may determine how his game resembles one of the entertainment games already on the market—a game called System Shock II. Transfer is key, the book's author says. 1107 Words.

os081112
In The Cards
Better to Play Games Than Do Nothing At All

The old man remembers something Confucius said and, with time running out, he considers the importance of cards in his game of life. Many kinds of cards come to his mind, from coffeeshop trading cards to cards that consist of summaries of essays he wrote. 1068 Words.

os081122
Art Buyback
My First Time

When his was purchased for a university collection, he regretted that it was no longer in a daughter's collection. Yet on the other hand, his wife and his other daughter each had one, so he was not entirely bereft of the picture. Months later, he got one. 564 Words.

os081202
Real Life Insurance
Looking ahead to seventy

The author, approaching 70—what he calls the age of wisdom—reconsiders the tired old notion of life insurance. He thinks what he would pay in premiums would be better invested in living. Death does not need to be insured, after all. It happens on its own. 1082 Words.

os081218
Gallery As Is
Marketing strategy for another kind of art gallery.

As he prepares to open his fourth neighborhood art gallery, he reviews the experiences of the previous three. One was in his condominium, the second was in an arts and crafts mall, and the third was a combination studio and gallery. As-Is may combine all. 1247 Words.

os081228
Drama and Choice in Emeralda
About structure in Learn Printmaking Online

According to Carolyn Miller in "Digital Storytelling," traditional dramatic structure has a place in interactive media. The creators of

"Learn Printmaking Online" have two tasks—using structure in game design and merging hands-on adventure in printmaking. 1046 Words

os090107
Substantial Characteristic Tension
Three Elements that are Mutually Reinforcing for Youth to Learn Printmaking Online

In Emeralda: Learn Printmaking Online, the author has in mind numerous characters he already designed and has more to come. Their dimensions are developed to varying degrees, but they all reinforce the mission, tension, substance and outcomes of the game. 873 Words.

os090117
Mi Universidad, Tu Universidad
Bringing the University Campus to your Home

The university persisted over centuries, a site-specific, virtuous experience resembling a citadel, a laboratory, or community center. States and societies cherish universities and going there a crowning achievement. Now this experience is going virtual. 889 Words.

os090127
ELPO Opportunity and Tension
Dangers in a Printmaking Haven

Despite that he's seen cartoons of bearded old men on streets with signs that say, "The End Is Near," this old professor thinks about the two-thousand scientists he read about who signed a five-part document saying just that. Can a game help save Mankind? 973 Words.

os090206
Game Levels and Writing Outlines
Similarities between Grammar Rules and Game Rules

Amid the goings-on in the life of a teacher who wants to work in both the online and the social levels of 21st Communities of Inquiry and Practice, the mechanics of writing with a computer, applied to game design, is the same as "level" in "outline" view. 1117 Words.

associate. Instead of making additions, he saves it as "official autobiography" and he makes changes to the original. 297 Words.

os090626
Teacher Movie
Entertainment Printmaking in the Age of Digital Reproduction

A printmaking professor thinks to teach printmaking as he learned it in the 20th Century to today's students is anachronistic. Printmaking is not frozen in time; it is the ancestor of digital media. So, he contends the teacher's role includes movie making. 1261 Words.

os090825
Hey Mom, There's A Card in the Toaster
Meditations on a Printmaking Challenge

As one of the designers for a blended online learning printmaking digital game I have the feeling I am playing the game while I'm designing it. It amounts to invention, in a way, or discovering the best strategy to win. This morning it's all about toast. 1413 Words.

os091004
Bellwether Brainstorm
Visions of a New School Coming

A persistent concept he calls the "perfect studio" seems closer today as the world economy presses for better ways to educate the young and re-educate the old among creative individuals in the mediums of printmaking. This professor envisions a new school. 982 Words.

os091014
Studied With
Asking for Higher Education with Individual Artists

A question was raised by a recent graduate from a college regarding advancing her education and her career, with a focus on printmaking. An apprenticeship? An internship? A graduate School? Institute? He addresses her last question, studying with someone. 1843 Words.

os091113
EATC
Electronic Artist Trading Cards

A chance meeting online with a creator of e-cards—those animated, musical greeting cards we get through our e-mail—launches this writer on an inquiry for some way to utilize the e-card in his inventing of a method for learning fine art printmaking online. 1181 Words.

os091123
Emeralda Works
For Me

When invited me to start a companion Diary of Making Emeralda, too, I started with the name. Emeralda is a blend of Seattle's market name, Emerald City, also the city in Oz. It's the name I submitted in a Northwest contest in '93 called "Name the Region." 352 Words.

os091203
Artist Stamp Collecting
Getting Started toward Electronic Artists Stamps

Working on his Stamps 'N Stories series today the artist realizes few people know what Artist's Stamps are, so he begins to write a descriptive pamphlet on the subject of getting started collecting these miniature works of art, planning to realize the eAS (electronic artistamps). 1147 Words.

os091218
About O'Studios
First day, Fourteenth Year

Fulfilling the requirement of explaining, on the first day here, what this island is all about, the author copies the description written six months ago during his work on the Emeralda Game bible. Pasting in the description, he next experiences O'Studios. 454 Words.

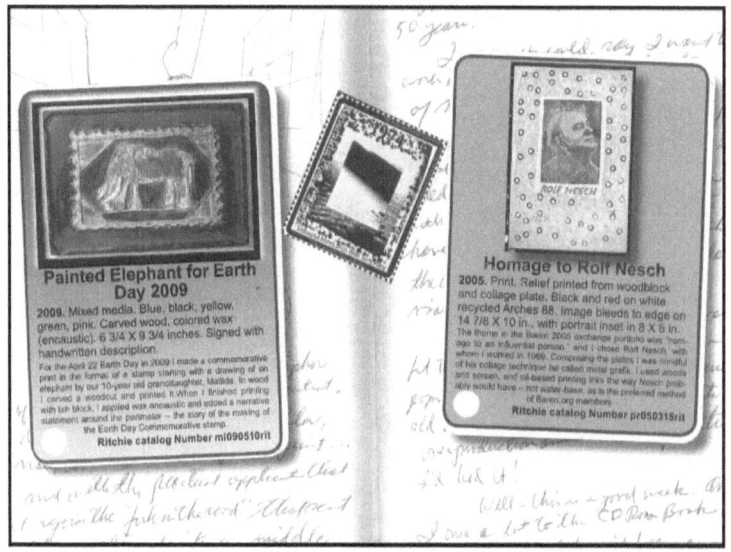

Painted Elephant for Earth Day 2009

2009. Mixed media. Blue, black, yellow, green, pink. Carved wood, colored wax (encaustic). 6 3/4 X 9 3/4 inches. Signed with handwritten description.

For the April 22 Earth Day in 2009 I made a commemorative print in the format of a stamp starting with a drawing of an elephant by our 10-year old granddaughter, Matilda. In wood I carved a woodcut and printed it. When I finished printing with ich block, I applied wax encaustic and added a narrative statement around the perimeter – the story of the making of the Earth Day Commemorative stamp.

Ritchie catalog Number ml090510rit

Homage to Rolf Nesch

2005. Print. Relief printed from woodblock and collage plate. Black and red on white recycled Arches 88. Image bleeds to edge on 14 7/8 X 10 in., with portrait inset in 8 X 5 in. The theme is the Basel 2000 exchange portfolio was "homage to an influential person." and I chose Rolf Nesch, with whom I worked in 1969. Composing the plates I was mindful of his collage technique he called metal grafik. I used woods and screen, and oil-based printing inks the way Nesch probably would have – not water-base, as is the preferred method of Baren.org members

Ritchie catalog Number pr050315rit

os100107
MOO Power
Harnessing human creativity in mediums-of-origination

Fifty years after his initial lessons in mediums of producing graphics, photography and text in his high school annual class, this author's sure it is the power of MOO (Medium-of-Origination) is central to multimedia arts—including computer game creation. 1949 Words.

os100117
Return to Emeralda City
Completing the circuit of ten imaginary places

It seems like a year since he wrote the Prologues. His Miller book is still near at hand. Things seemed to slow down and stop when he reached Video 'N Print in his way of organizing the 10 development steps outlined by Miller. Then what happened? Reality. 949 Words.

os100127
Your Mission
Four steps to game analysis and adaptation

The game inventor must practice every day with a four-part exercise in game analysis and adaptation. With a popular game by another artistic group (a classic rock group in this instance) he or she must complete four tasks in an hour or less and report it. 689 Words.

os100206
First Class
Consider this an online course

While completing a four-part tutorial he calls Mastering the Art of a Digital Game, the inventor considers offering his tutorial to people who invested in another one of his invention designs—a miniature etching press—which he believes to be interrelated. 426 Words.

os100507
Getting Dirty
Crawling around under a computer game

Inventing computer games is an uncommon and artistic process only barely understood even by people who have created something themselves. Computer games with which we're familiar are the visible but inventing them is like crawling around in a foundation. 264 Words.

os100606
Through the Stamp
Like the rabbit-hole

What some people call artist stamps are a kind of Cinderella—non-governmental issue stamps made by artists as miniature works of art, with purposes ranging as widely as there are stamp artists. This artist has made them for fun, beauty and learning games. 453 Words.

os100616
Hint Cards
Your hand

The inventor of a game to teach and learn printmaking steps cautiously toward teaching and learning the game itself. Like the image of a snake eating its tail; but not a hoop—more like a perspective on a spiral. He explains one of the cards he is drawing. 616 Words

os100706
Getting Started Writing PMC
Answers to questions

His idea is to co-author a book titled Printmaking Camp: A guide for printmaking camp leadership. He has a connection with a teacher in Texas who is interested. She pointed him to a useful blog site called Edublog, and so the dialog begins with questions. 263 Words.

os101218
Printmakers Commuting and Communing
Parallel worlds meet at the press

His innovative design of a miniature etching press is the secret weapon in a new kind of online game. He sees the combination—a real etching press and a virtual meeting space—as being similar to a joint-venture in a press release sent by Novel and the UW. 1025 Words.

os110127
After the Storm
From the eye of the hurricane

In the 1970s and 80s, an art professor with a penchant for trying new things, he was considered by one to be the eye of the hurricane. He attracted a small group of like-minded creative young artists from among students. Those days gone and the storm too. 461 Words.

os110206
Ghosts in the New Machine
Revisiting the idea through T. S. Eliot

This printmaker planned to write a series of books, culminating with "Ghosts in the New Machine: Between virtue and reality" but has yet to write them; in a famous essay by T. S. Eliot, he finds this poet/essayist has set down this same idea 90 years ago. 596 Words.

os110226
Phasing Emeralda
How Printmaking Roadshow changes Printmaking World

Reading about World of Warcraft, the massively multiplayer role-playing online game, the printmaker is reminded of his imaginary world when he sees the description of "phasing" in Jane

McGonigal's book, "Reality is Broken." WoW changes; so, too, Emeralda. 616 Words.

os110308
Rai and me
Taking a lesson from a little girl

Reading Jane McGonigal's book, "Reality is Broken," this teacher—who would like to teach printmaking in both real and alternate reality—comes to a part about a girl named Rai, and how she spends a day in her school life. He easily identifies with her day. 454 Words.

os110507
Video Art Docent
Touring an art show that has not yet been

An old art professor wrote what he thinks would be words and actions of an art museum docent for an exhibit based on video art in the Pacific Northwest, 1970-1985, from his private video archive of video tapes—the making of which he played a seminal role. 1801 Words.

os110517
Candied Dreams and Video Games
Box of chocolates and mapping the game

The last thing he recalls of the dream he was having before he awoke had to do with converting a boring bar graph to a mapped array of his ten imaginary islands in an imaginary artist's haven and awaiting him was an empty chocolate box for his postcards. 1180 Words.

os110527
Revisiting Oz
Copy Writing the Emerald City story

A favorite pastime of this artist is to take an essay by someone and over-write it with his own words, with remnants of the structure, like rebuilding a piece of cast-off furniture, or making an art object out of a found object embellishing his own ideas. 1387 Words.

os110606
Why Play Emeralda?
Revisiting the question ten years later

He wrote the essay in 2001, citing the parallel between a childish vision of flying and his own vision of role-play game invention. His routine these days is to check back ten, twenty and thirty years back into his journals—all part of his game, Emeralda. 602 Words.

os110616
Video dig script
Speaking to an imaginary audience

The author wants to ask for support in making an video art show. It's a show of video art in the old days, and he's the one who can do it. With support, he can make a presentation that's sure to win the heart of the museum director most likely to make ... 485 Words.

os110626
Warlords of Emeralda- Part VIII
Occupational therapy for printmakers

Eighth part of an essay, the author copies copiously from Wikipedia to meet a challenge from a partner in his quest for Emeralda game play; she said the game Puzzle Quest has game play qualities that can teach a wannabe-game designer, thus he copy-writes. 594 Words.

os110716
Funny Email in behalf of the SS United States
A message to SpinTop BizDev

He bought a video game online called "Escape from the Emerald Star," a typical Find Hidden Objects game. It caught his attention as the title included the word emerald, which of course is the root of Emeralda. It inspired him to write an email to SpinTop. 795 Words.

os110726
QR Code in Emeralda
Thinking of navigation

IIis interest in QR Code (Quick Response code) is piqued and he speculates how the system might be used in one of his Emeralda games. This example is using the QR code in the very important first element of Emeralda, the Elmer Gates Prize Calendar he made. 1453 Words.

os110805
Build your own Press Ghost
A flash of genius sketched out

He thinks his is a flash of genius: Sell etching presses to mature artists who then load the PressGhost with their own data, using the PressGhost template. The Halfwood etching presses are dropped shipped from Seattle's Halfwood Press Workshop and School. 190 Words.

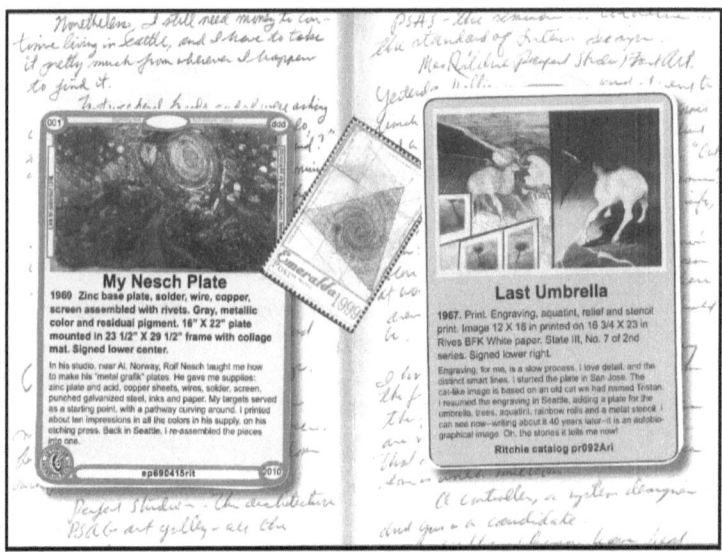

os110825
Firming up
It begins with the donut

You begin with the vision of a donut, writes the author, and a mandate: "Watch the donut, not the hole!" An artist in his or her senior years has accumulated huge resources in intellectual capital and tangible property, merged in the forming of the donut. 991 Words.

os110914

Twenty Steps to Prove Your Etching
Idea for a mobile learning game

He had a flash of an idea after he found there are very few learning games for mobile devices and, among these, even fewer which have to do with the arts. One game, Great Artists, caught his eye because it corresponded with a 20-steps list made on a grid. 450 Words.

os111003

What is Proximates?
The inventor describes his game

Someone asked him, when he mentioned Proximates, "What is Proximates?" and then he realized he had been using the word a lot, but he had never written out what it is. A food scientist would tell you proximates is what they call the food value of substanc... 1569 Words.

os111113

Escape Emeralda with Proximates
Considering the connection

Continuing his curiosity about the game, "Proximates," the author describes some potential connections between this game and "Escape Emeralda." Possibly it is a type of bonus for playing "Escape . . ." and relates to the adventure story about getting awa... 936 Words.

os111123

Boxes for Teaching Printmaking
How this creates jobs

The author writes about making boxes by hand for his printmaking teaching method. He relates hand box-making to the musical composer's creative process of writing a musical score. Making the boxes entails several related crafts: woodworking, joining an... 775 Words.

os111203

Ghost Readings
Allan Bloom and the Art Student

In the late 1980s the author and a co-worker named C. T. Chew started a project they referred to as "everything an art student needs to know" which would be published on a disc medium. One element was a collection of essential readings. This was to be it. 1434 Words.

os111218
If I had a Company
This is what I would do

Can one artist, who thinks he has entrepreneurial leanings, invent a method of doing business and apply for a patent for it? Would such a venture be in keeping with the artist's role? The author thinks Yes, it is, as artists today have an important quest. 984 Words.

os111228
Reading Rousseau
Reading notes from Emile

Reading notes from Jean Jacques Rousseau's "Emile Or Treatise on Education." (Prometheus Books. NY. 2003) It is recommended reading if you read the book "...the American Mind" by -----. P. 87. ". . . Ordinarily, the child reads the mind of his teacher much... 968 Words.

os120208
Bad Dreaming
Memories of a good job turned bad

His father's birthday today, and he's waking from another bad dream. What is this curse? Twenty-seven years after he walked away from the "plum of a job" at the UW and he's still having bad dreams about his time there. The dreams are populated with old n... 982 Words.

os120218
Rembrandt's Dream and Mine
Nails that stick up get hammered

He had a dream last night. It gave him a preview of what it will be like to be a confused old man—senile, one could say. He woke from one of those dreams they call "teaching dreams." It's a type of dream they say many teachers have after they've worked i... 1368 Words.

os120307
Rembrandt's Ghost Story Arc
What is the story arc of the book?
An art professor, on his way to a party, rubs an old printing plate and accidentally jettisons himself into Rembrandt's time. For a week he lives in 1660 Amsterdam, getting a close-up and personal view of what it was like be Rembrandt—the fallen art star. 641 Words.

os120414
Trophy Fishing
Winner or loser?
When he was very young he went fishing. It taught him there are big fishes to be caught, and this was the best thing to plan for when you go fishing. Trout or salmon, it was the same. The big fish was the object, and you planned accordingly. It seemed to... 1907 Words.

os120526
Working Alone
Why we are not rich - yet
A conversation illuminates the reason why, after eight years, his business has yet to show profits. He rationalizes, believing that it takes about ten years for a new product to be widely embraced and profitable, and this must be done alone and at a loss. 1406 Words.

os120605
Running a Trading Card Game
Collecting viewpoints
The trading card game owner-manager-wannabe surveys an article written by Rahenna, a person with experience, who posted a Website explaining what you have to do to manage a TCG. Rahenna, of Clavis, provided suggestions and a spreadsheet for planning TCGs. 1256 Words.

os120706
Arthur Koestler and the Perfect UI
Quest for a User Interface for printmakers
According to the first tutorial this writer looks at toward the making of a printmaking app of the kind he wants to associate with the line of personal printmaking presses, the ui—user interface—is the first obstacle he must overcome. Will this be a game? 1697 Words.

answers that occurred to him about some methods for doing this. 1279 Words.

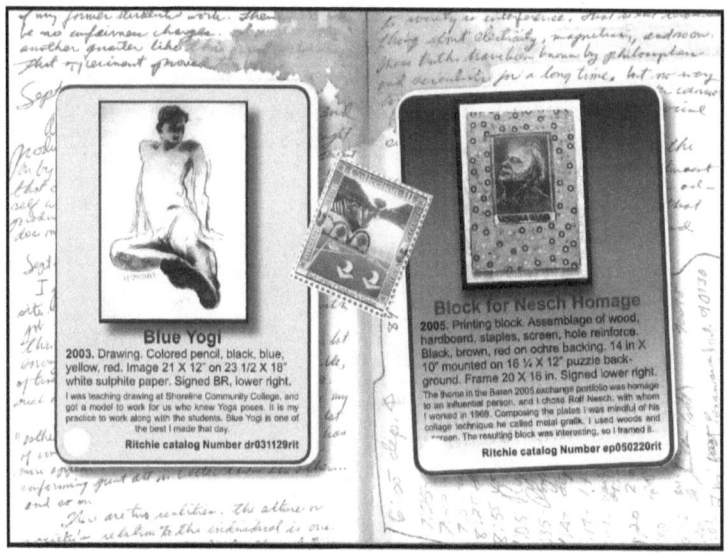

os121003
Why I am Like I am I Think
A meditation on selfishness

The artist got an email, the tone of which he'd heard before, suggesting if he would take advice when it's offered, solicit input from his "team" he might be surprised at the benefits he would get and solve his problems. The author thinks of all who help. 1244 Words.

os121112
MOOCs are Plainly an Opportunity
Industry notes that inspire and excite me

The art professor is excited by industry news which discusses the business models that might join with the Massively Online Open Courses being implemented, and Coursera is a leading figure in the essay. He extracts several lists which point to investment. 1161 Words.

os121122
Video Dig Reloaded Q&A
Fantasy Questions-and-Answers

Continuing his pursuit of a combined video art exhibition, a study collection, and a video game about video art, the author pretends he is in a Q&A session with a phantom group composed of people who might, thinking it is interesting, help make it happen. 2377 Words.

os130206
Moving on Wilcox' Advice
More about a press to make a game

Almost a month ago, Jeff Wilcox (CuriousGames) handed the author some free advice after Jeff had seen the WeeWoodie Rembrandt press and heard what this designer had in mind, which was to make a learning game. This is the third in the series that followed. 873 Words.

os130216
Desktop Assets
Management fifty-years in art with software

Since 1960—over fifty years ago—the author began making works of art in mediums ranging from pottery to video games. Now, at 71, he contemplates how computer software has been important in keeping track of this property of physical and intellectual kinds. 677 Words.

os130226
Be a Press Host
Sharing the printmaking experience

The designer of the Halfwood Press and inventor of the PressGhost SME feature that goes into the press is a teacher, and in this essay he dons his business man's hat and describes a new service for owners of the Halfwood press, based on house party sales.533 Words.

os130318
Public Art
Monument at Santander

He found an oddly-shaped tree log in a park, took it to his studio and made it a model for a public monument to be set on the Spanish coast in the city of Santander—all this as part of a fiction he created to launch his ship, the centerpiece of his quest. 567 Words.

os130328
On Community
The how, what, why of artist and community relations

For weeks Anne Focke and Carolyn Law, Seattle's sustaining sponsors of a salon called "What's Up?" have been sending their salon friends questions regarding artists and communities. The author considers the questions in light of artist's asset management. 1337 Words.

os130407
Why partner?
Ten reasons to team up for Video Dig Revisited

With an idea for a public art exhibit on early history of video art in Seattle, the author plans to realize the idea with the help of individuals and art education organizations and those who continue their involvement in cultural interests of the region. 1058 Words.

os130507
Organizing SSGI
Power of Limits

Writing a business plan for Seattle Serious Games Incubator, Inc. is not easy but it's fun—like serious games themselves. As one kid put it, "It's hard fun!" The author is about creating an organization chart, secretly imposes his tetrahedron to the task. 780 Words.

os130517
Young Rembrandts Metaphor
Copying Bette Fetter

The author adds support to PrintsCamp (printmaking camp), which is an idea he has nurtured ever since he designed a PTC (Parent Teacher Child) etching press suitable for learning the basics of printing and printmaking at home, after school, and vacations. 1658 Words.

os130606
Hard Times
Best of times

A moment of freedom allowed the author to comment on the times, after a long period of writing nothing about his plans because his plans seemed jumbled. Now, a new computer, an unexpected experience of revisiting his Rolf Nesch episode and his PressGhost! 368 Words.

os120616
Screen Saver
How I use a screen saver to sell preferred stock

He has a plan to convert art into becoming a special stock certificate called a Certified Convertible Preferred Share (CCPS), starting with the long task of converting images of the art into a database that identifies, controls, evaluates and distributes. 635 Words.

os130626
Fund purpose
A statement to use later

Funds will be for development and production of equipment, instruments, accessories, supplies, materials and services for online printmaking teaching, research, and practice. Equipment includes existing types and new designs, prototypes, experimental m... 110 Words.

os130706
Road Behind
Revisiting Bill Gates' book on future education

Bill Gates published, "The Road Ahead" in 1996. A commentary online addressed his remark, "education is the best investment." The artist/teacher studied this article and copy-wrote over and between the lines to make a case for starting a teaching company. 1471 Words.

os130716
OStudios Trading Card Game Blue Crown
A Trading Card Game by Bill Ritchie

Three-hundred fifty years ago a famous playing card producer named Jacques van Leest wanted the famous painter, Rembrandt, to print etchings as playing cards, but the artist was down on his luck, with no press until, like magic, a time traveler arrived w... 1967 Words.

os131004
Pay for the Ranch
Books about presses

The Shutterfly Photobook is a good way to preview the paper-based book for the Mini Press that would be the core of the business that provides printmaking learning games. It has a convenient deadline when special offers are made, is fairly priced on a re... 195 Words.

os131014
BizArtsKids
BAK is for winners

He thinks about the business of press making, feeling he has a tiger by the tail, and he wonders to himself, "Who will help release this tiger?" This business should be freed by kids to grow to the size of the market that needs and wants personal presses. 273 Words.

os131112
An Experience Business Model
Proposal for a virtual corporation

Etching presses are part of a business model which combines the tangible items (presses) with the intangibles of learning, social networks, and entertainment. Licensees who comprise the virtual business sell the presses and promote printmaking and prints. 145 Words.

os131218
A Thousand Little Indians
My concept offering to Riverside School

He has a concept to provide 1,000 Mini Etching Presses via Riverside School, a progressive school in Ahmedabad, India, which he discovered while watching a TED talk by Kiran Sethi in which she mentioned that there are 200 million school children in India. 1053 Words.

os131228
Never Quit
The most fun any printmaker can have

The most fun anyone who loves printmaking can have is to spend another day in a company where printmaking equipment, accessories and games are being designed, produced, taught, sold and serviced at the same time under a roof where printmaking never stops. 228 Words.

os140107
Press Reader
New frame of reference for Proximates

"We are all Proximates," he writes, "but we don't have a reader to learn about one another." He proffers a combination online magazine and network based on dynamic, worldwide printmaking as a social network linked to a miniature etching press he designed. 1109 Words.

os140117
Backstage Metaphor
What performance arts offer an online printmaking magazine

To plan an online magazine for printmaking, you need to go to your basic vision, which is that printmaking is a performance art as much as it is a visual art. To avoid the traps of using yesteryear's frames of reference, then, you need to look at theater. 1224 Words.

os140127
El Último Metáfora Proyecto
An online printmaking magazine

From this point in his life, he can observe back over seventy-two years and see fifty of them devoted to art, teaching and printmaking as his reason for being among his species and now he looks forward to an unknown number of years at an ultimate project. 1071 Words.

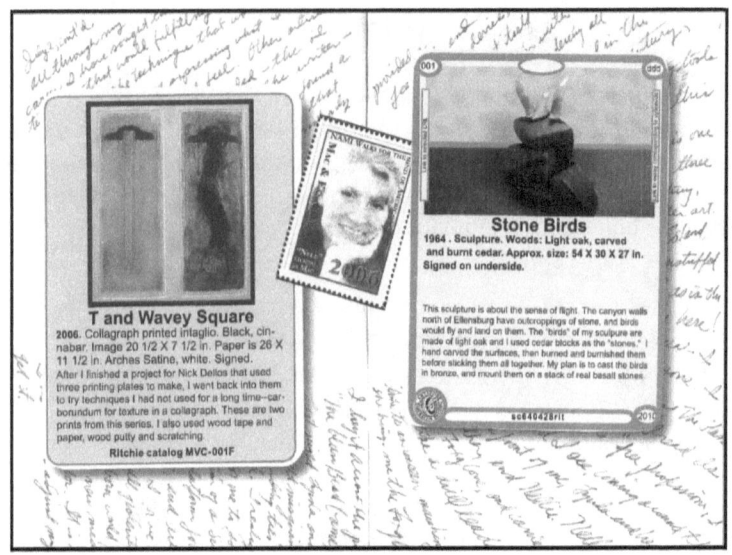

os140206
Moving Forward
From goods to services

He sends a letter of resignation to his readers as an exercise to map out a plan for the next ten years of his creative enterprise—the PrintmakingWorld On-line magazine. His vision is to maintain his original goals as family man, artist, and great teacher 1111 Words.

os140216
Printmaking Defined
Online magazine set to go

He wants to turn the switch to "on," as it were, and let the PrintmakingWorld online magazine go; but much remains to be done including the definition of what the printmaking experience is at its core. Printmaking is more than physical action in printing. 775 Words.

os140226
Social Ozine
The power of social networks and PMWO

It is appropriate on the imaginary island, Open Studios and Hospitality, to concentrate on the social networking value in the plan to start an online magazine for printmaking. After considering how games figure into the plan, social networking comes next. 674 Words.

os140407
Busker Etcher Story
A retail store at the Pike Place Market

Two etching press salesmen landed at a seaport with a cargo of etching presses and supplies, and both were expert printers so they knew they could sell by demonstrating their presses. They looked around, but no one had etching presses, and so no one was … 1018 Words.

os140417
Blog for Free Nomination
Many metaphors for my vision

You must send the URL to your blog / magazine article (should be accessible to all, and should be permanent!) before April 17, by 23.59 GMT + 1 so he could share this article with winners, send your magazine / blog article link to mediarepository@adesi... 1613 Words.

os140427
Print Theater

Concomitant strategy for the Seattle Printmaking Center

If you have ten years to do it, how do you build the Seattle Printmaking Center? It's the question before us in 2014 and demands an answer in a form understandable to the people who undertake the building of a center today through concomitant engineering. 270 Words.

os140527
PowerPoints Mine
Collected PowerPoint decks I made

He decided he needs to review the PowerPoint decks he has made over the past few years and assembles them into an annotated directory. Maybe this list will come in handy in the forthcoming months as he makes plans for his next decade's projects and goals. 974 Words.

os140606
Paying for Seattle Printmaker Center
My domain for an app

How could he raise millions to realize dreams of a Printmaker Center? The author is mesmerized by tales of huge profits that have come from making apps for wide distribution, and believes his concept app based on Rembrandt's Ghost will finance his vision. 860 Words.

os140626
Extensive printmaking
How technology transformed an art

What goes on in an artist's mind when he or she is at a time-consuming, slow task in making a work of art? Someone quipped, "Idle minds are the tools of the devil," because as artists' hands are busy making things, the artists' minds are likely to ponder. 1364 Words.

os140706
Founder's Story
From the horse's mouth

If he is to succeed in his plan to start the Seattle Printmakers Center, it may be that he needs his cofounders to know about him in as much depth as they need to know. It is important to know what he values most and how this core value relates to the ... 3249 Words.

os140716
BYO App Team
DIY App making

Sometimes you have to survive by your wits, and sometimes this is because you are a nitwit. To make an App is a prodigious task if, as they say, you are going to do it right. Apps are akin to making a work of art which, paradoxically, few are certain how. 1203 Words.

os150117
Take my idea, please
Searching for a takeaway

His survey of past Ignite Seattle speakers continues, looking for the takeaway that all 700 visitors would feel made the five-dollar entry fee and two hours' attention worth the trouble—like writing a high profile, high impact screenplay of a short movie. 543 Words.

os150127
Four beats
Ignite Seattle

Attending a speaker's coaching session has added new insights to his plans for a five-minute, twenty-slide presentation for "Ignite Seattle 26." Mainly, it was the brevity of stage presence that he learned, and that there is time only to offer four beats. 1137 Words.

os150206
Things look different today
The morning after

He went to yet another promotion for crowd funding at Perkins Coie, this one presented by Kartik Ram, where he met an attorney who had been an art major at one time. The press he lugged in was well-received and in the morning, things look different to him. 493 Words.

os150216
New school of printmaking
Based on the ancestor of all technologies

Imagine the school of printmaking at the Seattle Printmakers Center as being that which he started at the UW, which was deconstructed in 1984. In 2016, he can pick up where he left off, based on these premises: 1. Printmaking is the ancestor of all the d... 269 Words.

os150318
Steam Punk Special
Closing of the Pram Line of Halfwood Presses

With twelve unsold Pram Halfwood Presses, the author-owner goes on a brainstorming mission, to designing sales plans that combine games, online learning, and sustainability. His goal is to sell the dozen remaining Pram Halfwood Presses for goodness sak... 449 Words.

os150328
Go ask Media
Or a dolphin

A physical setback, a reminder of his physical limits, brings about a mood of deciding whether to go on with his ten-year plan to help build the Seattle Printmakers Center. Will age stop him? he wonders, and lyrics of many songs come to mind to guide him. 776 Words.

os150427
Death Defiant
Business plan for a life

A countdown begins for converting his assets to the Seattle Printmakers Center as the community asks for a business plan at every meeting—yet his plan is bigger than this as he forecasts the end of his old world and the birth of his new, more perfect one. 808 Words.

os150507
Mr Rembrandt's 47 rules
Fragmentary thought for a game

Mr. Rembrandt-the game-is based on the novel, Mr. Rembrandt. He used the game mechanics of Mr. Potato and Game of Goose for Mr. Rembrandt's game mechanic. It uses a game board, four pouches of tiles, each with two sides. One side has a part of a Rembrand... 162 Words.

os150517
My Golden Eggs
Value your customers because they are gold

Beginning to survey and update his database to connect with the business plan of Seattle Printmakers Center, Spc., the author reflects on the use of "Golden Eggs" as an expression to describe his patrons and is amazed to discover its use in "Angry Birds." 647 Words.

os150527
Regarding Tony White
Reminders, connections and questions

He began writing this the day after Kathie Flood and Birney Mitchell visited his studio and she mentioned that Tony White works at AIE. He was slow to recognize the name, but then it came to him, he stopped at our booth in the Edmonds Art Festival in 20... 656 Words.

os150706
Proof reloaded
Movie notes recovered

Recycling a notepad one day to make a fake book titled, "Loosey's Tale" for a snapshot, the writer found some penciled, barely readable notes that he thinks he wrote that looked like the lyrics to a song or lines from the 2005 David Auburn movie, "Proof." 821 Words.

os150716
Four arguments for cultural arts districtification
The elephants of Uptown

The author walked through the Seattle Center to discover a DOTA-2, major eSport event in progress. Thousands of Millennials convened, an international crowd like Bumbershoot, Bite, or Folklife, and impressive for the $18 million in prizes for the winners. 1698 Words.

os150726
What if Uptown is NOT a Cultural Arts District?
Asleep in Seattle

After a month of steady work educating himself on why his neighborhood, Uptown, could or would be designated a Cultural Arts District by the City of Seattle, he awakens after 30 days asking if the whole idea is an exercise in political and economic games. 1682 Words.

os150805
Beachcombing
Subject

Games wash up on the beach. A crate washed up today with dozens of boxed copies of a game titled, "Rembrandt's Selfies: Ghosts in the new machine." The rule book is in a foreign language. Only the title and subtitle was in English, and he supposes if h... 516 Words.

os150815
My assets for a game
Turning artworks into games

"My kingdom for a horse!" Shakespeare's King Richard III said. He thinks of this as he works for a game, probably a collectible trading card game, that he can use to exchange his assets for his dream, his Perfect Studios—a setting where he can teach, res... 782 Words.

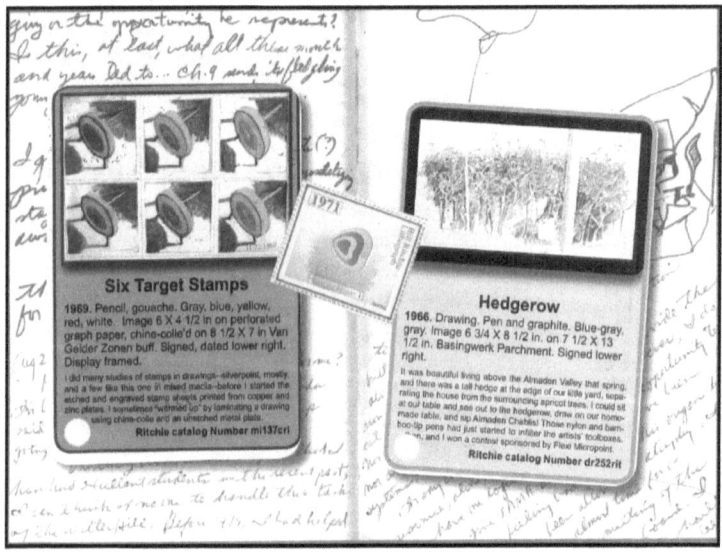

os150825
Printmaking and Multimedia
Four ways to succeed in printmaking today

The founder envisions a multiple-platform publishing approach to the futures of all people who love prints, printmaking and printmakers. Printmaking World is a suggested magazine title for the Northwest Print Center and Cultural Arts Technology Incubator. 1549 Words.

os150904
Goals of an Emeralda Warrior
You must escape Emeralda

When he leaves Emeralda City for ArtsPort, and all goes well, he can make the complete circle of the islands, end up at Video N Print, having thus completed his Year of Living Copiously, mastering all the Domains of Expertise, and a good way toward the... 378 Words.

os150914
Artists Collectible Trading Card Design 101
A method for Asset Management and Legacy Transfer

His goal is to link the properties of a provenance of a work of art, artist's book, artist trading card, or any kind of ephemera or memorabilia of interest to supporters and investors of the Cultural Arts Technology Incubator, a benefit corporation that ... 2323 Words.

os150924
Not your usual IPO
Unveiling a new model of art

In a world that is rapidly changing for humanity, artists have a role to play. Like some large game, intermingled among industries and polite social groups. In a structured world of teaching he learned this and taught what was sustainable and extensible. 1232 Words.

os151004
Mr. Rembrandt
Toy and game for Kickstarter

Bill Ritchie invented Mr. Rembrandt, a toy and board game with parts, screws and tools one needs to build a tabletop Rembrandt Press. A 64-step pathway on the game board determines the parts for winning by answering questions on collectible trading cards. 1146 Words.

os151014
What I want
Banking on one's IP

With 1.5 million Americans interested in a printmaking experience, he wants to exceed their expectations by giving them something you would expect from a great and good country, the USA. He can do this in Seattle with a factory and a school based on his ... 503 Words.

os151112
National Art Patron Bank
Making your deposit

A comment from the creator of Scenario Engine generates a test for this artist, examining how a certain work of art he created is to be deposited as an artist trust holding. At the point where he is scanning the work in sections, he finds a game of cards. 1463 Words.

os151122
One hit could do it
Emeralda Warrior to the rescue

With childlike enthusiasm, the author wakens from a dream about printmaking, a vivid dream of what could be happening with the NPC&I. He hits on the solution that has been eluding him for years: How to make a board game with the WeeWoodie Rembrandt Press. 1116 Words.

os151203
How I learned to stop worrying
And love my game

On any given day he plays his game of life called "Emeralda: Games for the gifts of life." It's a game about freedom in an America of prisoners after a century of faltering educational institutions has led to where ignorance and vulgarity have taken over. 420 Words.

os160206
The Intern
What do you say to do?

A suggestion from the co-founder of Busker Etcher is that people would be willing to help the Northwest Print Center & Incubators get started if it could be clear as to what tasks need to be done. The author writes off-the-cuff to describe the first task. 1189 Words.

os160406
Thinking about Marq Dean
Inventory of a designer's work

Who is Marq Dean? Singer, composer, a songwriter? Or producer of films, digital artist? The list of accomplishments of the Google search "Marq Deans" is long. After the author finally met Marq is that he is the producer—the sum of many talents and skills. 789 Words.

os160416
How much would it take?
Estimating startup costs of Sip 'N Print

A visitor to the Mini Art Gallery preceding the coffee hour printmaking session asked the question, "How much would it take to start up?" - a general question about the Northwest Print Center Incubators. The author considers his immediate task, an empt... 973 Words.

os160506
Coming to terms
Tired and lonely but not giving up

After two years of working toward the Northwest Print Center Incubators, basing his premise that the Halfwood Press would be his legacy and sales of the press would provide not only a substantial income stream to support the center's activities but provi... 678 Words.

os160526
Catch the new wave
Subject

While working with a particularly tricky piece of software as a part of producing a teaching video the author felt like he was lifted, as it were, like a surfer lifted by an auspicious wave. He felt for a moment like an employee of the Ritchie Foundation. 258 Words.

os160605
Education Art
Putting education first

The author taught for 19 years at the University Of Washington School Of Art where he found the art education philosophy flawed, and in 1985 he set out to develop "education art" based on the fundamental difference between printmaking and its sister arts. 767 Words.

os160625
Join the Printmaking World Investment Club-8
Chapter 5: How much does it take?

An enterprise in the Northwest Print Center Incubators means that the founders provide the business structure and establish what each brings to the table—experience, or money, or tools. The question, "How much more capital do you need?" must get answered. 1118 Words.

os160715
Theme in Printmaking in a Box
Inspiration from Columbia University

On the program "Sci-Tech Now," the author saw teachers at Columbia University teachers College, bringing new technologies to the art ed classroom, a new certificate program on creativity. The goal is like his: To mix traditional art with new technologies. 643 Words.

os160725
Printmaking in a Box
Scripophily for an alternative to art ed

"Pixar in a Box" is taken as a metaphor for the author's ambition to invent the printmaking teaching method for online and hybrid delivery. He cobbles together financing plans and mimes the structure of Pixar's example and thus escapes from old world w... 376 Words.

os160814
My world for a game
There is a game in us—let us begin

He has been dreaming of a game for many years—perhaps decades—he calls a "children's game," for reasons he can only guess at. Now, in his sunset years, he thinks of a quote attributed to a Chinese philosopher: Better to play games than do nothing at all." 390 Words.

os161003
Akira Kurosaki in Seattle
Remembering influences

Akira Kurosaki touched many lives of artists, teachers and students in the Pacific Northwest. The author remembers them well, especially since he had an interest in video art—and therefore Akira touched his life in a way additional to his printmaking w... 1165 Words.

os161122
For the kids
Building legacy

When his wife and he had pre-school age kids, they thought about their future. He even drew up a timeline, plotting the ages of their daughters from the years they were born, and he charted what he hoped would be his career and, hence, how he would provi... 523 Words.

os161218
Winning is not the greatest purpose
It's the only thing

He's trying to come up with new purposes for the making of the printmaking club of his dreams, and as he tries to see the club through the eyes of prospective members, he thinks winning is the only reason to join any club, the only purpose that is needed. 1524 Words.

os161228
Creating a memoir in the age of digital reproduction
Old wine in a new bottle

The 1964 book, "The Act of Creation," by Arthur Koestler influenced the author's decision to create a memoir in a fashion unlike the book form so commonly taken up by people writing their memories. A new approach is taken because the readership no longer exists. 1176 Words.

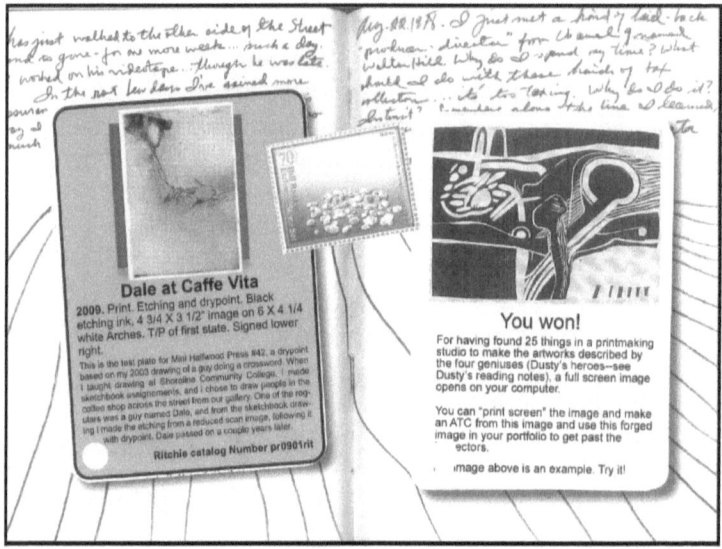

170407
Valuation of John Dowell Jr
A tiny element for the IPCIW

Following his meeting with Rick Hooper, with plans to meet Maria Bariantos regarding development of first floor spaces in new housing projects in Uptown, he came across a videotape of a performance by John Dowell, Jr. and he saw this as one of the elemen... 151 Words.

os170417
Why Batelle should meet with me
Science, research, creativity and community

Battelle is a research group, a "think tank" and scientifically oriented to solve the world's problems. Not only in scientific research but in social problems as well. Social problems, like scientific problems, require creative problem-solving skills. Cr… 1378 Words.

os170507
Vision of myself as an old man building a model ship
A passing ship, a passing thought

The old man sits over his cluttered tabletop, and in the center of it, a model ship. He is restoring the Emeralda, a ship borne out of his imagination—a creation of his artistic mind. To say he is restoring it needs clarification, for it is not the Emera… 129 Words.

os170517
Slumdog millionaire inspired Art Action
Suspense and the destruction of a legacy

In the movie, Slumdog Millionaire, suspense built all through the movie because the quiz show was worth millions, and it was uncanny how the character played by Dev ___ always knew the right answer. In his vision, such a drama might result around the dis… 415 Words.

os170527
Why invest 25,000 in real estate?
Brains, brawn and interest rates

Taking out $25,000 from savings and putting it into a real estate investment (REIT?) for the purpose of development of a cultural center makes sense. The dividends may be intentional—and does not take away significantly from their family. If anything it … 841 Words.

os170606
Tiddlywiki my autobiography
Considering an onyx apple

He is writing his autobiography, and he has been at it for about four months. He works on it every day—sometimes all day—when he is not corresponding with people about printmaking and his Halfwood

Press line. When he tells people about it, he's probably ... 705 Words.

os170616
Did I touch your life?
Considering the creative place maker

Today he will meet a neighbor in Uptown, and he is asking him for advice on how to further his goal to contribute something of lasting value to the City of Seattle. What he knows is that their City has problems which the government and its people would l... 827 Words.

os170706
What is in the name Krajewski?
Dwelling on the game Eco

He likes to learn as much about a person as he can before he meets them face to face and his plan is to meet John Krajewski. He is co-founder of Strange Loop Games, developer of Eco, a kind of EarthSafe 2022 game. As he drilled down with his name he foun... 2574 Words.

os170815
A new approach to artists' assets and legacy transfer
Borrowing from other professions

An old friend—and he means old like him—asked about ways to catalog his art, he thought about his method. It's a good one. He tells stories—that is, he writes stories—about the works. Then he puts it in his autobiography. Once it's there—picture and stor... 493 Words.

os170914
Why Emeralda Works
Ambiguous, like the enterprise

Emeralda is the name of an imaginary place, like Hogwarts University or Oz. It's where I retreat to spin my intricate web of business ideas. The Internet, AKA, the Web, is the virtual world for the kinds of business ideas that work for him. As for him, h... 450 Words.

os171924
Too complicated
Taking a tip from NAMTA

That's the reaction he gets when he describes the Northwest Print Center Incubators. First of all, the core of this business development proposition is printmaking, which in itself is complicated. It is complicated because it's an art form, but even in t... 373 Words.

os171208
UE printmaking virtually
User experience and a song

Once the viewer QR code is scanned on your phone, then the APP will download, it requires almost 50 Mb. Then scan the QR code on the press, and this will open your lessons. This is a new kind of cooking show—except instead of passively watching cooking, ... 313 Words.

os171218
Artiscripophily
Revised version

It is the future and he has lived into it. As a boy he read about the future, saw pictures of what science fiction writers envisioned what was to be. Much of it has changed from fiction to reality. Much of it still is still to be realized. His boy's imag... 1180 Words.

os171228
Microsoft HoloLens in education
A chasm that takes a leap of the imagination

How would you like to see the art department at the UW be closed? How would you like to see the UW Medical School closed? If we had only enough resources to keep one of them opened, which one should we choose to keep, even though it would mean closing th... 825 Words.

os180107
Anatomy of a virtual press
Premonition of the Martin Schneider design

In charting the history of the WeeWoodie Rembrandt press, in this episode they examine the list of owners and their back stories with the intent to create a VR printmaking experience beginning with the end in mind of forming an international club made up... 446 Words.

os180127
Ten reasons why I write my autobiography
Getting ready

Seven-hundred pages into his autobiography he feels he's hit a hollow spot, a slightly dead feeling and he's having a time getting into the first two and the last one of the eight book he planned. The words of T. S. Eliot come back to him, "We shall neve... 866 Words.

os180206
Should my autobio be a Zine?
Reflecting on a year of writing a memoir

After a year of writing and preparing images for his autobiography, shaped like a boxed set of eight hard-bound books, he came a difficult place. The first twenty years of his life are hardly worth writing about, let alone expecting people to gain anythi... 623 Words.

os180216
An unexpected development
The day I sold my best painting

An old friend stopped by the other day and asked how much his painting was. He told him – off the top of his head - $3,750. He saw a table next to it. "It says here $850!" "Oh, well. That's . . .." He was thinking the label was put up by his daughter and... 1080 Words.

os180407
Where will I go?
Options for 2019

You need an office to go to, an office alongside some other people who are striving to do something new and creative, something profitable, something of lasting and global value. You could try to get a job at the Bill and Melinda Gates Foundation, but th... 234 Words.

os180427
Dumb hope of farmers and artists
Two worlds of politics

His father had the dumb hope that someone among his children would carry on the farm. That way, despite the hopelessness he saw every day of his life, when his sweat and tears seemed for naught, it would prove successful in the end. If not by the time he... 403 Words.

os180517
Norwegian Independence Day
Remembering a time in 1969

In 1969, Lynda and he struggled across the median of Karl Johann's Gate to catch a shuttle to the airport. He was weighed down with a wooden box containing the plates he made at Rolf Nesch's studio and at Atelier Nord, Anne Breivik's workshop. Hurrying b... 638 Words.

os180527
Prisoners of the mainstream
A young painter's odyssey

Yesterday a visitor came and they had a long time to reflect on their positions. They had met two years ago when she was partway through her training in a classic painting school. This year she graduated, and ready to start her career as a portraitist. T... 599 Words.

os180626
What value?
Mining for equity

He searched for two missing files – that is, he thought they were missing. He back-tracked to the folio containing the prints designated by the file numbers on the screen. He found the folder. Opening it, he found the prints with their numbers that match... 313 Words.

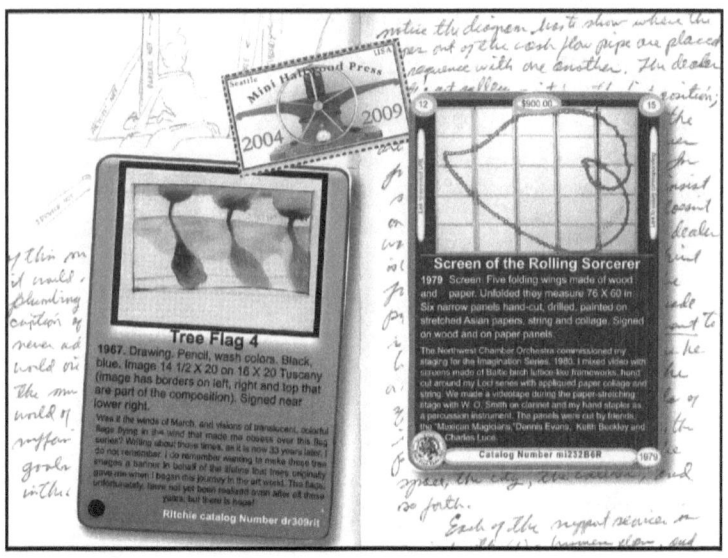

180706
Mined games
Artists Rest In Peace with artistrip

Shuffling my files as he works on his Catalog Raisonne, it seems like a scavenger hunt. This may be a clue. They tried some escape games, and they rely on clues and puzzles. If his art is to be converted to artistsrip, then it may be a clue to engage p... 290 Words.

os180805
Wacko Press Lender
Pros and cons of buying Halfwood

Barbara bought a press in 2009 for $676 and returned it for resale in 2018. In the nine years she owned it she never used it, she said. It sold for $1,000 and he will charge her $200 for my labor and he will charge the buyer $75 for shipping, handling an... 498 Words.

os180815
Appropriate esthetics
The Age of Feuilleton revisited

Daily he checks in to social media and he finds his former alliance with the arts of questionable circumstances. Hermann Hesse described it as "the Age of Feuilleton" It was an age of intellectual frivolity. Feuilleton is a French word which refers to th... 689 Words.

os180825
My kingdom for a partner
Alone again naturally

He was reviewing the website under construction and he wondered how the user could understand what to do – this or that choice? Which one would lead to success, which one would be a blind alley? Another person working with him might see the answer immedi... 294 Words.

os180904
A day in the life of the IPCI CEO
Corresponding with Reka Nemet

It is hard to read with your eyes closed; however, in the arts – such as in popular music like the Beatles', ". . . living is easy with eyes closed . . .," it can be done. Suspending one's fears of the unknown, suspending reality for the moment, eyes clo... 1762 Words.

os180914
Why I went to work for the International Print Center
Incubators
An article worth copying-over

In a glance he knew Alan AtKisson's story was his. It was written by a Swedish civil servant, but he could have written it from the viewpoint of a worker for the International Print Center Incubators, or IPCI. With a few small changes, it was his story o... 2039 Words.

os180924
Why artistscrip is not a Ponzi scheme
Responding to an unasked question

It's all about the future, the illusion of calculation – a phrase he made up to compare drawing perspective with people's hope and fear of the future. In drawing perspective and elaborate use of color in painting, the illusion of deep space on a flat pla... 980 Words.

os181113
Hayter's book for a back story
Thoughts for a STREAM game

Having collected in the time of three days – November 9-12 – numerous responses to his Hayter Game concept, it's time to take the next step toward making the game part of STEM to make STREAMS – Science, Technology, Reading, Engineering, Arts, Math and ... 626 Words.

os181123
Where do I go from here?
Plan for a Meetup

On November 21 he wrote: "The future of printmaking hangs in the balance. Come to Printmaking Tuesdays at the Mini Art Gallery, a Meetup at 812 5th Avenue North, C-2. Meet friends, talk about the future, present and past of Seattle's printmaking scene lo... 362 Words.

os181218
Philanthropy Reimagined and the Hunt for the Wee Press
The many faces of build-a-press

In his game, Emeralda, players must cobble the events of their days and seek to understand how they fit. For example, Sean Elwood, founder of Art Estates, left clues on the Web which will help him contextualize his day's activities. His posts led him to ... 1859 Words.

os190107
In these times
Printmaking is therapeutic

He began to read an article about the brutality of these times, how stress can be mitigated by taking up a craft. It said those which have repetitive actions are especially therapeutic. He places printmaking among these because one inks and prints a plate... 979 Words.

os190117
When art is not art
Reflecting on art for the 21st Century

He went to a pop-up exhibit and panel discussion sponsored by MIT Northwest Forum, and several other sponsors (who sent money to the main sponsor). It was called "Art for the 21st Century." He was reminded of a biography of Richard Feynman, the physicist,... 753 Words.

os190127
Why I play Emeralda
A day in the life of a Gates Prize Winner

Emeralda is a structure for collaboration. It's a discipline for readiness to collaborate. Playing Emeralda every day, in every way, makes his mind ready to see opportunities, in hope they will appear. Simple things give him hope that an opportunity is co... 407 Words.

os190206
Legacy Logic
Education of the young

As he sorts the images in their project, he thinks of the logic behind it. The images are only good for two things, and that is education of the young and the pleasure of the old. His favorite people among the old – people over thirty he guesses – are tho... 455 Words.

os190216
Proprietary search engine
A game of the mind

Playing with numbers – entering six digits with a two-letter suffix – finds him a five-page article he wrote in March 2000, about a colloquium held in Ellensburg sponsored by the Washington State Arts Commission to collect data about art education here. H... 635 Words.

os190308
The old man leans back
Art student fantasies

The old man sits down in his favorite easy chair and reaches for his pipe and tobacco. He fills it, lights up and leans back. His canvas is in front of him, glistening with freshly-applied paint strokes, bright in the morning light filtering in over the n... 1068 Words.

os190318
Teach Emeralda
Steps toward setting up the game

Lately he has been reviewing his game and how he plays it. The name of his game is Emeralda: Games for the gifts of life. It takes different forms – sometimes a board game, sometimes a search game – like a scavenger hunt – sometimes, like this, a stimulus... 526 Words.

os190328
Structure for collaboration
A life insurance policy for hope

"A structure for collaboration is like a life insurance policy for hope," said Rosabeth-Moss Kanter. If printmaking were not therapeutic, he wonders if he would not be in such great health? His mental and physical health is good and it's partly because he... 752 Words.

os190407
Programming for ArtsEd Washington
Eight-hour day job

Asked what area I am interested in by the executive director of ArtsEd Washington, he responds with one word he chose from the three that she offered: Programming. What does it mean? Not computers, certainly. Washington State ranks 46th in arts funding, s... 375 Words.

os190417
Bee Press
How to ship a press to Africa

For years he has dreamed of teaching printmaking worldwide. Fifteen years ago, this dream showed a sign of coming true when he designed a personal-sized and beautiful, all-purpose hand printing press. He sold them in twenty countries, but the most elusive ... 575 Words.

os190427
The importance of provenance
Proof

He reviews a conversation with an African here to study marketing her honey in the USA, a rambling conversation and reference to the importance of the Uniform Resource Locator, or URL. Reviewing this plus trying out the search engine, the importance of ... 479 Words.

os190507
A diamond from Botswana
Her story

He has received her story in trust. A woman from Botswana shares her life story with this teacher as part of their plan to collaborate on developing communication between her country and the USA and beyond. Through trading honey for things of value and to... 365 Words.

os190517
Reason 4 ARTISTSCRIP
Fittingly Sustainably and Developmentally

Fourth in the ten reasons for ARTISTSCRIP – after considering the fun of it, the gamification potential and the recursivity of this approach is its fit with the United Nations Sustainable Development Goals. In a sense, recursivity is proved by this. He th... 511 Words.

os190527
Legacy logic revisited
Augmenting scripophily with a real case

Having captured a quip from an African entrepreneur, he reviews her simple statement of purpose as her vision of the logic of turning American art collectors into investors in her enterprise – Chabana Farms, a farm collective in Botswana. The stage is set for ... 650 Words.

os190606
Mavis speech
From the ghost writer files

They were about to go onstage at Seattle's Impact Hub, a center for workplaces, a university and business accelerator which offers a lunchtime "Lunch and Learn" program weekly. They were to make their presentation together for the first time. She called... 724 Words.

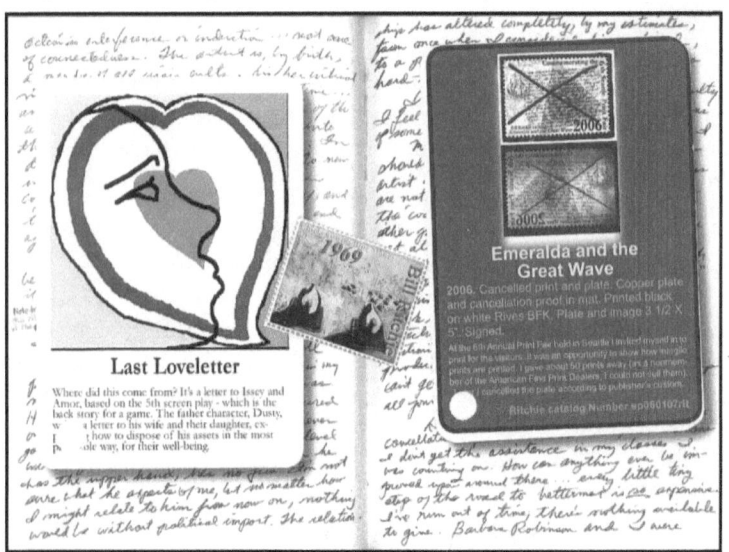

190616
My app Emeralda
Not for the 20th Century

To use a popular expression – so popular it's become one of the catch phrases in movies – he made an app for artists asset management and legacy transfer. It's only in his golden years – at age 77 – that he realizes that's what it is. Unlike the mainstrea... 328 Words.

os190626
What are we waiting for?
When all the news is bad look for the good news

The author believes the many sayings about the power of the individual to change the world, but he thinks also that it begins with changing one's self. Scanning the news of the moment online, things look bad; but the worst thing that's happening is the w... 745 Words.

os190706
Testing Erin Jeck's Ten-steps
Twenty-one days on O'Studios

Open Studios and Hospitality – he asks how he's doing. He has one idea for opening his family's art studio and gallery suggested by the speaking coach Erin Loman Jeck. Her advice is to buckle down and create an opening for a one-man show of Carl Chew's ar... 150 Words.

os190716
Reviewing artistscripophily
One year later

A year ago the author wrote a paper explaining the background of his invention he calls artistscrip, derived from the hobby of collection old worthless stock and bond certificates. Finding it during a routine checkup to find if anyone else used the term held a ... 806 Words.

os190726
Linking Artistscripophily to Artopoly
Stages of an invention

For two days he has been playing with the ARTOPOLY game principles to link them to artistscrip, his invention to link senior artists' legacies to fundraising altruism, education and family sustainability. Thus far the results are encouraging. This essay should... 279 Words.

os190805
WIFM Etching MOOC
In the frame of Davidson Galleries

Considering the experience the author had recently at the Davidson Galleries when he met several printmakers ranging from the boomer generation to Millennials, he considers what is in the Etching MOOC for them. Taking each person, he tries to imagine the... 173 Words.

os190815
Nuggets and diamonds
Discovering truths by review

His task is proofreading essays dating back ten years for their project they call Ritchie Mined. One morning he found several nuggets, like diamonds in their backyard, one of them (ap100424) suggested a way to combine our artworks with a game he calls artistscrip 159 Words.

os191004
Emerson's morning warning
Fear and procrastination

The first message he finds on his screen in the morning is a quote by Ralph Waldo Emerson: "What you are afraid to do is a clear indication of the next thing you need to do." He has a list of things he needs to do, and he's afraid to take steps for fear … 176 Words.

os191014
My Life To-do list
Cards on a table

He spreads his artist trading cards on his table – a reminder of things to do. Every time he enters his family's Mini Art Gallery on 5th Avenue North on Queen Anne Hill, he's confronted with a big green tabletop where he puzzles out the meaning of his li… 282 Words.

os191024
Glimpse of Emeralda
The example of Bea Gold

While updating a few pages of O'studios' 'Zine directories he is impressed with the need to tell how he does this, and why. Partly it's because he saw a message from Bea Gold, a 90-something artist who has been making prints it seems like forever. She's … 483 Words.

os191103
Script for Build-A-Book
How to make a book in Kindle Direct Publishing

When the author opened his eyes to art, he was looking at a virtual image of it on his smart phone, an image of a virtual artist trading card, also known as artistscrip, one of a deck of four cards he purchased. It was in the format of amazon's Kindle eB… 285 Words.

os191113
Mystery of Kalahari Honey
The Iron Springs meditation

He arrived at the Iron Springs resort in the middle of May 2019 and was reminded of the time like this three years ago. He remembers that was the year he was told by doctors he would not walk unless they operated and installed titanium rods in his back. … 827 Words.

os191228
Year of hope
The bottom of Pandora's box

The end of 2019 puts him in the mood to think about the coming year as he pays for his business license with the knowledge that Emeralda Works will continue to be a legal entity, although maybe the last year of its existence. What signs are there to have hope? 558 Words.

Quantity of O'Studios 'Zine essays

When we began formatting the 'Zines for publication as indexed books in 2004 the number of 'Zine entries was slightly over 2000 nested in 117 Mb on a computer. Our daughter Nellie Sunderland joined in the task of organizing them and, by the year 2019, we listed thousands more with 568 essays attributed to *O'Studios*,' the *Island of Domains-of-expertise in Open Studios and Hospitality*.

Afterword

How and why 'Zines?

My version of 'Zines goes back fifty years to when I was a college student at Central Washington State College living in my art professor's rental. Her collection was so big she had to keep part of the books in this old house - a tall, skinny structure built at the turn of the century. She had rows and stacks of volumes in an upstairs room. I could browse in my professor's library any time.

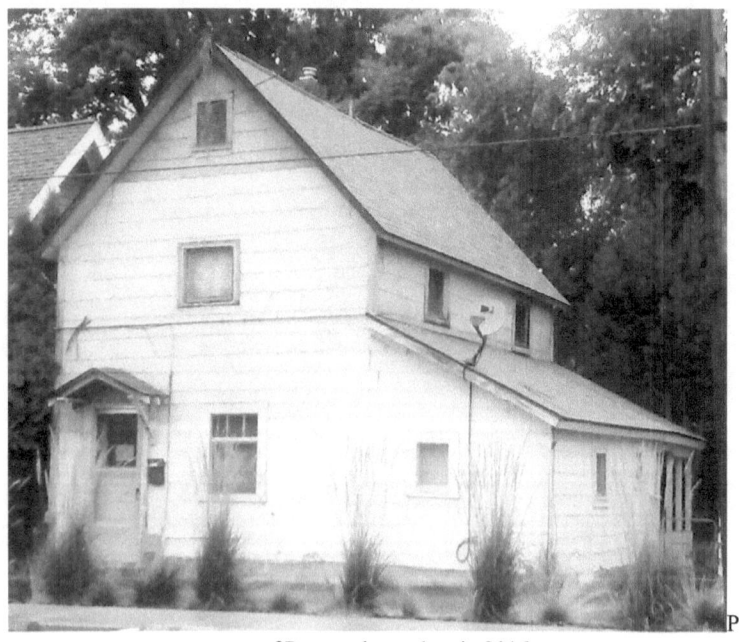

Photo of Purser place taken in 2016.

My professor, Sarah Spurgeon, named her rental *Purser Place* after one of her favorite students, Bob Purser. Bob was a year ahead of me. When he graduated, the privilege of renting her house was passed to me. I lived in it while getting my BA in arts and crafts.

Born and raised on farms in the Yakima Valley, I had never known anyone with a personal library! I had made a goal to have a library like that. A few years later I got a master's degree and a position at the University of Washington. By the 1980's I had a rather good library, but smaller. Following Sarah's example, I shared mine with students and they shared theirs with me.

Looking back, I wonder what became of Sarah's library. What happens to professors' libraries when they retire and pass on? She died in 1985 – the same year I resigned from the UW.

Access to Sarah's library and its value to me inspired me to invent a new and better way to access professors' libraries. Today, teachers do not need a room and shelves for their books thanks to computers. It is not only for their books they can give students access. A digital library can also give insights into a teacher's mind.

Who cares what professors think?

What effects can teachers' libraries have on their students? For example, did Bob's and my access to Sarah's library influence the fact that he and I both became university art professors? Being in the right place at the right time gave Bob and me access to Sarah's library. We saw a piece of her inner sanctum. It was a rare privilege.

Following that undergraduate experience, I went to San Jose State where I studied with Geoffrey Bowman. Here, again, I had access to this professor's private library. Even more, I had access to his lithography studio – complete with a stereo and LP collection!

My way, the Information Highway

The age of digital reproduction changed things for students and also for people who are not formally enrolled students, thanks to the Internet. Anyone can enter a teacher's virtual inner sanctum if these teachers digitize their writings and reading notes.

Technology makes it possible so everything that a professor writes and records in their teaching career can be in their *cyber library*. Their mass-produced publications would be listed in online bookstores of course; moreover, now unique, unpublished articles, private journals, recordings - audio and video - diaries, manuscripts, screenplays, and miscellany can be accessible. These used to disappear in the age of mechanical printing when the professor retired, lost their mental faculties, or died.

Dead Professors keep on Teaching

Sixteen years into my college teaching career, I experienced an awakening that changed my life as a teacher. I was on sabbatical in 1983 and driving across the country with my family. We stopped in Montana to see friends in Polson, near Flathead Lake. My mentor's late brother, Arnie, had been a retired art professor like my mentor, Reino Randall. Arnie died working on their dream home.

We visited Arnie's widow at her home was on a little island connected to the shore by a short bridge. Their daughter offered us a tour. As she opened a door to a small, windowless room, she said:

> *"This is where Dad kept his things.*
> *We don't know what they are."*

I stuck my head in to see. Instantly I recognized what it was: forty years of teaching, research, practice, and community service. Boxes of slides, portfolios, sketchbooks, files burgeoning with notes and unpublished articles crowded the shelves. All this was resigned – imprisoned like Alcatraz - in a room on a rock in Montana. I thought:

> *"I have a room just like this!"*

Arnie's daughter's words have been imprinted on my brain since that day.

Techno-teaching

As a student of Sarah, Reino and Geoffrey in the 1960's, added to a generation of media technologies under my hat, my legacy wouldn't have to end up that way. Not *this* art professor! Contact with artists in their sixties, seventies and eighties - like Rolf Nesch, Stanley Hayter, Maria Guaita and others - taught me the value of teaching artists' life work.

Since 1968 I had been journalizing my thoughts on art, printmaking, and technology. In 1979 I started using an Apple II-plus, to digitize my reading notes. After thirty years they are on hard drives, on the cloud and blogs. Nuggets of ideas are online for anyone curious enough to mine my data.

Teachers can keep their brains alive with the aid of computers - which is partly what this 'Zine Index is for. In the 1990's, when electronic publishing was the way to future documentation, my ideas were no longer confined to private journals and diaries. With on-demand publishing, I make books. I've come full circle; my personal library is on paper as well as digital. Ten years ago, I summarized 344 essays for the first edition, the 2009 O'Studios 'Zine Index. By now, for the 2nd edition, there are 568 summaries.

For online study

My purpose in creating *Ritchie Mined* is to give future online art students an opportunity to pick-a-professor's-brain. In the old days of the 1960's, students raised their hand and asked questions in a classroom setting; or, sometimes they'd have a chance encounter at a store or a coffee shop, in a small class or a seminar, or worked one-on-one with the professor as a graduate student or assistant.

That's how it was for me. Opportunities for picking the professor's brain is sometimes the benefit of higher education. Teachers are wellsprings of knowledge; but opportunities to share are rare. Professors may publish their work online, so students don't have to purchase expensive books. On the web, students can read a teacher's blog, which is something like picking their brain.

When I was a professor at the UW, I had another eye-opening experience that proved to me the value of writing things down in the off chance a student might want to know what I read. It was the 1970's and I was reading topics outside of printmaking. I made notes on three-by-five cards. By my fourth year of teaching, several boxes with hundreds of reading-note cards sat on my bookshelf.

I showed these little boxes to students in my printmaking class and, to my surprise, a student asked if she could borrow them and take them home. She assured me that she would take good care of them. She was a teacher, too, so she knew how valuable they were to me.

When she brought the boxes back, I opened the lid and saw little slips of yellow note paper bristling from between the cards. She wrote comments and suggestions for further reading, with remarks like *"Wow!* and *This is so TRUE!"* It was almost talking over coffee.

From that experience I learned some students are interested in learning more about my knowledge than what I can share in class. They want more than what the syllabus offered. They want to drill down into their knowledge base and mine their professors' thoughts. I was like that, and I was lucky I could use my professors' libraries.

It was recently I saw the term *mining information.* Picking someone's brain means *mining someone's database of knowledge.* There are mountains of knowledge in a human mind, deep wellsprings of experiences and some wisdom. Looking for gold or diamonds, one mines for nuggets of wisdom or bits of glittering knowledge. In a perfect world, some students *mine* teachers' minds and they may need maps of teachers' knowledge base.

In the 'Zine Index project, my goal is to open doors to mine my knowledge and experience without my presence. I have been writing my ideas, concerns, hopes and, sometimes, anguish, in journals almost daily for fifty years. In this book are their subject lines of text in my journals, on computers, or transcribed videos.

A day in my past life

My UW career peaked in the 1970s. I had a lot to say, and all the means to express myself - even on videotapes! I could describe a typical day in my printmaking classroom as *exciting.* I recall day in the middle of the morning etching class in one of the department printmaking studios. At the same time - across the hall - students were working printing on lithograph stones.

One of the etching students brought me a zinc etching plate she was working on to ask a question. But she had to wait while I explained to someone from across the hall to ask me why her lithograph was printing too light.

Meanwhile, in a corner three students were fiddling with a video setup and one called over to me: "Mr. Ritchie, is this tape cued?" holding up an open, reel-to-reel videotape we used to tape a demonstration about to start.

It was the girl with the etching plate's turn, and she asked me, "How do you do it? How do you keep track of all this?" Amid these print productions, experiments in video art, she wondered how managed addressing myriad issues without going crazy.

I said, "I pretend it's like a radio dial. I tune in to something—teaching, research, practice, or service—and focus on it. Like changing channels." I took her plate and put my loupe on it. "Your plate is etched enough, yes."

Yes, it was wonderment: in one room people were experiencing *teaching*, *research*, and *practice*. I loved it, especially if, as it happened on occasion, a visitor wandered in for a look - there was also *service*. The four were happening at the same time, or *concurrently,* under one roof.

As for me, amid this hurricane, I was in the eye; I was calm, because I loved it. Here were the four cornerstones of university life: *Teaching, Research, Practice* and *Service*. I came to call the *TRPS Principle* that supported the edifice I knew as the University at its best.

Across the campus was the UW Hospital—a renowned *teaching hospital*. I'd read about the *concurrent* approach to medicine that started in Scotland in the mid-1700's. I hypothesized that the same approach—teaching, research, practice and service - could be taken in art. I called this notion, "Perfect Studios."

My notion of *concurrency* took shape slowly, as I had no idea where this path would lead. Maybe, if I had known that it would end of my career at the UW Art School, I would not have stepped onto this pathway. Concurrency works in med schools and teaching companies, but could it work in art school? The jury is still out.

My formal teaching career lasted nineteen years. My first working study experience abroad in 1969 initialized changes. Foment of the '70s in America rippled through everything, as there was the American war in Viet Nam, Civil Rights movement and environmental worries. The times were changing, and I wanted to change with them. *Perfect Studios* was the right idea, the right time and here - in the Pacific Northwest - was the only place open to me to search for it.

Architecting Perfect Studios

To design my Perfect Studios, I went inside myself and examined my career. I thought about my successes and my former students' - successes owing to diversity of expertise. I made out ten skills with the newest multimedia technologies alongside the oldest printmaking methods. Public speaking, teaching, computer graphics, and other domains-of-expertise all connected, overlapping and complementing one another. These ten could serve as a working platform for a new printmaking curriculum!

If I were to actualize this, then I needed proof to justify promoting the change. In 1982 an opportunity came to make a tour of printmaking and electronic studios *around the world*, and I took it. On a sabbatical, my mission was to gather proof to convince the faculty and administration of the UW art school that a sea change awaited our students. The next Millennium was near.

The art faculty rejected the notion of blending printmaking with new media. It was 1984, after all, just like George Orwell described in his book. I resigned the next year. Unlike the medical school across campus, the art school was not the right time or place to model a concurrent teaching, research, practice and service.

I left the university to search for my ideal vision of "Perfect Studios," environment suitable for art students who would practice in the 21st Century. I wanted something similar to a teaching hospital (or teaching company) where the four pillars of higher education in art would support one roof, as it were.

Mapping *Ritchie Mined*

I missed campus life, especially the students' input. I was learning as much from them as they were learning from me, probably. There were short teaching gigs at The Evergreen State College and the University of Oregon, but there were no places to reform printmaking education. I was out of time and out of luck; I was just one more itinerate professor cut loose from a campus, no place to call home. Just another Bozo on the bus.

152

Since there was no real university for me anymore, I made one up I dubbed *Emeralda Communiversity* in an imaginary region north of Seattle. Over the years, on the basis of TRPS and my hypothesis of ten domains-of-expertise in a printmaker's education, I architected a school distributed on islands in a gigantic lake for these domains. Listed alphabetically, *Open Studios & Hospitality – O'Studios* - is the fourth in the series of 'Zine Indexes.

A reader might imagine being on one of the islands and coming to a teacher's cottage in the woods like *Goldilocks and the Three Bears* but instead of finding bowls of porridge, there's a library. Browsing through the teacher's journals and computer files, one would find something like this index of ideas and musings indexed for the ten-based platform.

How the 'Zine idea came

Once upon a time I sought to publish online magazines for our printmaking video mail order business. There were alternative magazines - *'Zines* – people published both in paper and online. This was before mainstream magazines went online. They blended comics, magazines and graphic novels.

I took the name *'Zines* because – having burned my bridges to institutions - I lost the associated validation of publishing in academic journals. To store and retrieve the text quickly, Emeralda's ten imaginary islands gave me an indexing system. My 360-day calendar, like an itinerary touring the islands, structured them chronologically making it easy to execute searches, back up and upgrade or migrate them as technologies changed.

The ten-based indexing system was to structure my long-range goal to teach printmaking online - which, by the turn of the century - had become my mission in life as a printmaking art teacher. *Ritchie Mined* may not be an improvement, and it's no substitute for facetime, but can be something different and possibly more fun.

What's next?

Recall that I left the brick-and-mortar institution in search of an environment where teaching, research, practice and service are concurrent. How does *Ritchie Mined* fit in this model? The potential of this for online teaching is unknown – yet to be tried and tested. It's of no monetary value that I know of.

I sort of fell into new media by accident, thanks to the UW audio visual department and computer center. I was lucky also that I had a wife and family to help me sustain and manage my database and collected works. Amazingly, even those boxes of reading note cards are still in my family's collection and are moving to hard drives and the cloud.

My hope is to connect these data to an online course in printmaking. The relationship of my musings to making prints is unclear, but art must have *content* as well as *form*. The links between content, i.e., what's in an artist's mind with his or her etchings and woodcuts are hard to see; or, maybe they don't exist. Maybe we have to make them up, like artificial intelligence.

I think creative art is a blend of intuition, faith and technique. Printmaking is a special case of art technique because printmaking is the ancestor of all information and communication technologies, i.e., the means by which we experience most of the world of the arts. In addition, printmaking has qualities of a performance art. Printmaking is a *process* art, a *time-based art* form with a social value. Prints are artifacts of a happening, a moment.

We live in a time when it's possible to make a blended online printmaking class, my most avid hope. Besides printmaking techniques - which are available on the Web - students can access this professor's inner visions and link content, process and form. A paperback or Kindle E-book may not be enough, but for me it's a beginning, a way to make possible the mining of one's thinking.

About the author
Bill H. Ritchie
Education

Born in Yakima, Washington, 1941 and attended public schools in the Yakima valley. Attended Central Washington State College (CWU today) 1960-64, graduated with honors with a Bachelor of Arts in art and crafts. Married Lynda Fisher and moved to San Jose, California, where he attended San Jose State College (SJSU today), majoring in printmaking. Graduated in 1966 with an MA and immediately started teaching at the University of Washington School of Art in Seattle.

Professional

Hired as an Instructor, he worked with Glen Alps, noted printmaker and professor at the UW, Bill was promoted to assistant professor in 1969, Associate in 1974, and full professor in 1978, started the west's first Video Art course. Speaking engagements put him in touch with world printmakers and he circled the globe in 1983 on a fact-finding survey to help justify redesign of a printmaking curriculum to include electronic and digital aspects.

Unable to do this at the UW, he resigned in 1985 and took his research into the community. He continued learning multimedia software and hardware he started. Roaming the region's resources, he sampled everything from interior design to hypermedia and the Internet.

Interested in the social aspects of printmaking and crossovers with other professions, he experimented with joint ventures, even using his skills in dentistry as an assistant in both oral imaging systems and setting up front office computer systems.

Crisis

Environmental concerns surfacing in the 1970's and 1990's with such figures as Al Gore and the *Union of Concerned Scientists* put art education in a new perspective for Bill and he launched a personal mission, *EarthSafe 2022*. On this model he contrived to

155

start a movement, pressing art education into alignment with science and Earth stewardship.

As printmaking is the ancestor of all new communication media, he changed his worldview of prints, printmaking and printmakers. As distance learning developed, he set about inventing a platform to use serious games in combination with face-to-face workshops known as blended online learning.

He changed his focus away from college-age and career-bound populations to the youngest and the oldest learners. Today he applies his fifty-years experiences to the design of affordable, small printing presses to go with such a course if he succeeds.

Today

Ritchie and his wife, Lynda, still live in Seattle, where she has opened a family art gallery to display his life's work and he has a workshop. Their married daughters live nearby, the older Billie Jane Bryan working in corporate food service and the younger, Nellie Adelle Sunderland, assisting with Bill's writing and graphics—including this production of *O'Studios 'Zines Index: Ritchie Mined.*